Title: JUST MY OPINION – Letters to the Editor
Author: Arland R. Meade

Cover Design: Toni Weel
Book Layout & Text Design: Toni Weel
Photo Front Cover: Tom Meade

ISBN 978-1-312-30404-8

First printing, August 2014.
Second printing, June 2015.

Printed in the USA by Lulu Press.

Published by Toni Weel. Bartow, Florida.

Special thanks goes out to one of Arland's "human readers", Toni Weel.

She has had the pleasure of reading to Arland over the years.

This collection of editorials is due to Toni's connection to Arland and her work and desire to make it so.

Arland's children: Tom, Chuck, and Melody Meade. We thank you, Toni.

JUST MY OPNINION

Letters to the Editor

Why Do I Write Letters For Publication In Newspapers?

An urge to communicate may be a partial explanation, but there is more. When I read or hear statements by leaders of our nation, or notice their actions, I feel I can serve a little by looking further into the subject. I often see a need to call attention to a related factor that is not expressed or is flawed.

I do not contradict for the sake of contradiction; I often point out ridiculous or damaging statements and acts that in some way do harm. One example: just before we invaded Iraq, I wrote, a satirical letter stating that if we sent a Piper cub to Iraq we could haul out all the weapons of mass destruction. Not believing me, our administration invaded Iraq at a cost of a trillion dollars and several thousand dead Americans, and found no weapons of mass destruction. At least I had the satisfaction of being right.

I do not know whether I believe in intuition, but sometimes so called "evidence" just shouts the opposite. So I try to find words that expose the truth as I see it. This works with any subject, from international affairs to a defense of the word "snuck", and to a national drive for funds to buy underwear for military veterans. For my letter about the underwear, I received a phone call that I should leave this country. As a veteran myself, I declined.

I have indulged in these letters to the editor off-and-on most of my adult life, but more frequently in the latest fifteen years. As I am 99 years of age, maybe I think that I have acquired more wisdom than I have. But rarely has a newspaper declined to print my offerings. This includes newspapers in Vermont, Massachusetts, Connecticut, and Florida.

A friend suggested that these be compiled and be made available. Many are no longer in my possession, but several are. So here they are.

Arland R. Meade

TABLE OF CONTENTS

Letters are by date - newest to oldest.

Paranoia, Texas-style

They who blame Obama for everything have yet again shot themselves in the foot.

The recent "news" from Texas gave the "blame everything on Obama" gang an opportunity to look stupid in front of the whole nation, again! Now how could the Commander-in-Chief have leaked that the Federal Government might use these "military training exercises" as a means to take over the state of Texas? He even let a map of Texas be released, and leaked a statement that some fifteen hundred Army Special Forces are to start military maneuvers in Texas and perhaps Utah.

The ever vigilant new Texas Governor, Greg Abbot, was on his toes. He reported that he had alerted the Texas National Guard to "monitor" the federal movements to make sure that the U.S. troops did not take away civil rights and other rights that Texans cherish. Furthermore, he, supported by U.S. Senator Cruz, from Texas, revealed that the federal government has huge military and prison facilities deep under several Walmart stores, with deep tunnels linking them. Even a couple of candidates for the Republican nomination for President of our nation have added that this matter should be looked into.

Our nation has more than twenty military facilities in Texas. One of them is reputed to have more troops than any other nation has in any one base. If President Obama were not so poor at keeping secrets, he could release these troops on Texas by a call or telegram. Instead he leaked the fact that fifteen hundred Special Forces were to engage in war games.

So is this "exercise" a ruse of a clever Obama, or is it an example of former Vice-President Dick Cheney's opinion that Obama is "the worst president in my lifetime"?

ARLAND R. MEADE

Published: the Lakeland Ledger 5-18-2015

Teasing the Pollsters

The election is over; people voted their preferences. The results tell us that Congress should show its gratitude by erecting a plaque twelve feet tall under the Capitol dome stating "Americans love this Congress".

Once in the voting booths, we the voters renounced what we had been telling poll-takers over the past several years, during which we repeatedly rated Congress lower and lower until even the infamous "do nothing congress" that President Truman railed against looked much better. Voters this year had so little respect for Congress that on election day they reelected the same members—and, to boot, added a few of like mind when incumbents declined to run again.

This remarkable vote surely proves that Americans in their wisdom reversed positions come Election Day. They had been only teasing the pollsters; they really preferred "the party of 'No'".

Some Americans think that Americans deserve who and what they vote for. Think about this during the next few years. Therefore, our beloved Congress should immediately require the United States Postal Service to create and print first class stamps bearing the words "I love Congress." Then every time we affix a stamp we can smugly pat ourselves on the back and recite a nursery rhyme's last line "Oh, what a good boy am I."

ARLAND R. MEADE

Published: the Lakeland Ledger 11-14-2014

2

All That Stability in Mideast

As we compare the Middle East of a dozen or so years ago and now, do we notice how much more democratic and more stable it is now? One American economist has calculated that our wars there have cost us several TRILLION dollars—without setting any valuation on the more than six thousand American military personnel killed and who knows how many crippled or brain damaged for life. I have not heard any estimates on how many residents there have died or have been crippled.

In spite of all the good these wars have done for the Middle East; some American leaders want to spend more billions in more help, such as training armies to maybe fight somebody. Apparently the job is not done. What is the job anyway, and whose is it?

By the way, I worked in Iraq for more than a year as information officer for our technical aid program. My pay checks were from the U.S. Department of State. In those days, before we "stabilized" the Middle East, Americans were welcomed in the stores and were often invited to have tea. Few women covered their faces in public. A few Muslim and Christian women even held Iraqi government positions.

I am sure that the Iraqi residents are thanking us for bringing stability and democracy to them.

ARLAND R. MEADE

Published: the Lakeland Ledger 9-30-2014

Being Attacked by ISIS

A few - I hope only a few - senators are warning that ISIS (Islamic State) is growing so powerful in the Middle East that it is a threat to our American homeland. At present ISIS is a self-declared Muslim Caliphate in a small barren part of Iraq and Syria. It wants a nation governed by their version of Sharia law that, for example, favors punishing adulterers by stoning to death the woman participant - but not the man.

An Islamic army is being recruited so that this Caliphate may by the sword expand. If expansion succeeds, ISIS will have opponents on all sides. It will be sufficiently occupied in defending itself that its adherents will have little energy left to attack the United States. Of course terrorists can originate in any part of the world, Islamic or otherwise.

In the U.S., alarmist trigger-happy persons like Senators McCain and Graham want to inject more military action, which would likely as history has demonstrated, create a reaction of more, not fewer, persons who want to harm the United States. I wonder where Graham and McCain think that the ISIS air force will strike us first, or which port the ISIS navy will enter first, or whether the huge ISIS army will invade our homeland through Canada or Mexico. Will all three invasions happen at same time and overcome our feeble military forces?

Several decades ago I lived in Iraq, working as information officer for the technical aid program commonly referred to as President Truman's Point Four. I do not know whether this experience influences my decisions now, but I do believe that we should let the Iraqis and Syrians produce their own successes or failures without further military interjection by the United States.

ARLAND R. MEADE

Published: the Polk County Democrat 9-6-2014

Teaching to the Test

Much is reported of teachers condemning state-mandated tests of students, or the number of them, claiming that teaching what some state officials think students should learn ("teaching to the test") is taking time from what the teachers believe they should be teaching.

If it really is harmful for students to take state tests on what a council of administrators believes they should be learning, in, say algebra, those tests should not be administered. Many teachers say they know what to teach and to test better than the administrators do. Who knows best? Let's get the evidence.

Perhaps teachers could cover both what they and the state board believe the students should learn. Life is full of tests, and I do not believe that those I took in school harmed me. All teachers give tests to check on how well the pupils have learned, and sometimes to gauge what changes in methods might be adopted. So these teachers teach to their tests. Do they think that "teaching to their tests" is damaging?

Student scores on standardized tests is of course only one of the factors in evaluating tudents, teachers, and schools. But they can help. I recall that many decades ago my daughter in a good high school in Connecticut told me that her mathematics teacher talked a lot about a variety of subjects but taught little of the subject she was employed to teach.

Perhaps if the state had mandated that she "teach to the test," her class might then have stood out as deficient and been a candidate for remediation.

Perhaps my daughter would have had a better career if that teacher had taught to a state Comprehensive Achievement Test. But my daughter is now the principal of an elite private school in Washington, D.C. What a sneaky way to avoid being forced to "teach to the tests."

ARLAND R. MEADE

Published: the Lake Wales News 6-25-2014

U.S. Has Paid a Painfully High Price for Blunder in Afghanistan

Some American politicians and others are proclaiming that our administration should never have released five Taliban soldiers that we held at Guantanamo and especially not in a swap for an American soldier held prisoner in Afghanistan. Our stated reason is that these just-released Taliban leaders want to kill Americans. Of course they do.

If we were in their boots, so would we. The urge for revenge is natural. The Taliban ruled most of Afghanistan when an Arabian gang called al-Qaida used American civilian airplanes to attack critical buildings in the United States. The Taliban neither planned nor participated in those attacks. The Taliban did, we can assume, make a mistake in allowing the Arabians led by Arabian Osama bin Laden to live in Afghanistan to scheme against the U.S. Bin Laden's Arabians' planning could have been done in Saudi Arabia, Egypt, Yemen or elsewhere.

Perversely, the United States decided to attack the nation of Afghanistan, not Saudi Arabia. When the United States invaded Afghanistan, the Taliban Party and others fought back. Did that include killing Americans? Of course it did. If an Afghan army or air force were to invade the United States, we would willingly kill Afghans and, of course, not consider ourselves terrorists. I will not join some Americans in saying that exchanging five Afghans for one American was too high a price. But I will say that we have paid a painfully high price for our blunder in occupying Afghanistan.

ARLAND R. MEADE

Published: The Lakeland Ledger 6-24-2014

6

Should Ukraine Follow the Lincoln Principle?

Many Americans believe that when the Ukrainian government was confronted with the secession of Crimea, it should have reacted the same way that our President Lincoln did when our Southern states seceded. Lincoln ordered the Union army to invade the South. He believed that the voters of the South choice of their own government was not valid – that the national borders took precedence. That decision led to the bloodiest war ever on this continent. Homes and families were ruined and hundreds of thousands of soldiers died.

The situation in Eastern Europe is similar in principle, but the conditions are hugely different. Let's imagine that the Ukrainian government threw its entire military power into Crimea to crush the area that wanted to be independent or part of Russia. The government decided that the rights of its Russian speaking area must not interfere with a national boundary, whether that boundary was logical or a mistake. Would America and other powers accept this because Lincoln did this?

Whether any amount of negotiating would have prevented our Civil War, or will prevent a war over Crimea we can't know. We do know that civil wars historically have ended only when one side utterly crushes the other. The Spanish Civil War almost a century after ours is another example of this.

Will the decisions of nations satisfy everyone? Of course not, but any deal will be better than the death and destruction that would result from an application of the Lincoln precedent. And people on both side of the Ukrainian border can keep their homes and lives.

ARLAND R. MEADE

Published: The Lake Wales News 5-7-2014

We Don't Need a 'Level Playing Field'
At the Cost It Would Require

Often I hear a politician or purported economist complain about our trade imbalance with China, usually along with the assertion that we need a "level playing field" with China.

We can, but we won't, level the playing field. To equalize the playing field we would have to legislate that wages in the United States would be no higher than those in the lowest-wage Asian country.

Then we would abolish or reshape our retirement plans and our Social Security program to be level with those of, say, Bangladesh.

Of course, we would abolish labor unions, work-safety rules and inspections and pollution regulations so we could breathe smog as thick as in north China.

With the playing field thus leveled, American-made goods would be at least as cheap as those from China and our closed factories could reopen.

Most dock workers and ship crews could be added to our unemployed people until they moved to our newly created factory jobs at the new low wages.

How many Americans would be willing to vote for any politician who openly advocates policies, such as the above, which would really accomplish this "level playing field" ?

Would you?

ARLAND R. MEADE

Published: the Lakeland Ledger 4-30-2014

Gun Control

Over the past year, I have heard many interviews, discussions and recommendations about gun control. Typically, they begin with shock over the mass killings, especially the murder of schoolchildren in Connecticut. Then the speakers immediately say that, to prevent these, we must keep guns out of the hands of criminals.

Wrong target. Make a list — it will be very short — of these slaughters by any person with a criminal record. Except for the know-it-alls who get radio or TV time, one will discover that these killings were all or mostly committed by individuals with no criminal record.

Criminals will find ways to get guns, but those criminals are not the people who use automatic weapons to kill groups of innocents in schools, churches or colleges.

The individuals to be recognized and treated, or at least to be kept free of guns, are those who are mentally disturbed.

Even if we had the Wisdom of Solomon, we could not identify them all, but that is the direction we should travel.

Another approach would be to outlaw automatic weapons and conduct a never-ending search for them.

Yet another would be to repeal the Second Amendment, on which the supporters of such guns wrongly depend. That amendment had a good purpose in America's first century but its utility is now long past.

ARLAND R. MEADE

Published: the Lakeland Ledger 1-22-2014

Iran Leads the United States in Peaceful History

Over the most recent 175 years, Iran has been far more peaceable than the United States of America.

From our invasion of Mexico in the 1840's, the U.S. has fought in about seven major wars against nations that had not attacked us nor credibly had the intent or means to do so. We have initiated several military incursions that one might call "mini-wars." Our only true war of defense was against Japan when Japan attacked us at Pearl Harbor.

During the same 175 years Iran has been the aggressor in one war, a dispute with Russia over territory. It has fought several wars in its own defense, against various nations including Great Britain and Russia.

If we believe that past actions by nations are predictive of future actions, then the world has more to fear from the United States of America than from Iran.

Now is a good time for Iran to mount a campaign to get all nations to eliminate atomic weapons.

Affairs between nations are seldom dictated by fairness. Iran of course feels that it is unfair that it lives with atomic weapon nations on both sides: Israel on its west and Pakistan on its east, yet we condemn Iran for even considering making its own.

If atomic weapons were abolished, Iran would not be tempted to develop them. The whole world would benefit.

Would the United States and Russia agree to abolish their atomic weapons? Of course not, but Iran would at least set a peaceable and history-based precedent.

ARLAND R. MEADE

Published: Lake Wales News 10-26-2013

Friend of 'Mine'?

I 'literally' agree with the Frisbie essay on the overuse and misuse of certain words and phrases, such as 'My head literally exploded.' (Democrat, 'If not us, whom?' Saturday, March 29, 2013).

I here present a word use that I cannot justify or explain: several friends including two with Ph.D. degrees also could not. Perhaps S.L. Frisbie will 'ask the world' to help me.

Universally we hear people say 'He is a friend of mine,' 'They are friends of ours,' and the like, with other personal possessive pronouns.

I understand 'He is my friend' and 'He is a friend of me,' (rarely heard, although grammatically correct), but what or who is the 'mine' referred to?

Something that is mine, I own. I can say 'That car is mine,' or 'This house is mine,' or possibly (Forgive me ladies) 'This woman is mine.' Now which of those possessions might the speaker be the friend of? A friend of my house, of my car, or of my woman? Or has he something else of mind when he uses the possessive pronoun?

Those sentences are nonsense, but are used by every speaker of English that I ever met or listened to. We all know what the speaker intended to convey. He is communicating, but how did such absurd grammar get into our language?

Whoever can explain this to me will be my friend but please, not a friend of anything that I own. However, he could be a friend of my friend, if that is his meaning.

ARLAND R. MEADE

Published: the Polk County Democrat 4-6-2013

Concealed-Weapon Training

Recently The Ledger published an editorial about the issuing of permits to carry a concealed weapon ["Concealed-Gun Training: Improve Florida's Standards," Jan. 24, 2013]. The number already exceeds a million in Florida. The editorial listed some requirements for this, including a training session to make sure the weapon carrier knows how to handle the gun and to shoot it accurately.

This bit of training does not put me more at ease. But at least when a person pulls out his or her gun for self-defense or the opposite, he or she is more likely to hit the person intended. If I irritate a neighbor enough that he pulls out his concealed gun and shoots at me, I am comforted to know that he will kill me and not bungle the shooting and kill the nice next door neighbor who is picking a rose at the time, or, perish the thought, shoot himself in the foot.

Knowing that so many Floridians carry concealed weapons may make us into a more polite society. Why aggravate somebody who might have such a weapon on his or her body?

This nation is likely to get some new laws about licensing and registering weapons. Most of these will make schoolchildren or theater-goers or college students safer. The outlawing of and determined search for military-type rifles would cut such slaughter from dozens to a couple or so per incident.

Our slavish following the words of the Second Amendment in our Constitution may keep our legislatures from outlawing military-type weapons. It is time that we start the long procedure to revoke this now-stupid and dangerous Second Amendment.

ARLAND R. MEADE

Published: the Lakeland Ledger 2-11-2013

Keeping Our Eyes on the Target

Felons are not the persons who are doing the mass-killings of children and others. We do not need to keep felons from getting guns in order to make our school children safer. Our targets should be elsewhere. The shootings in various gatherings have been done by young white males with no criminal records. They surely have brain defects.

Perhaps we can pass laws and establish screenings to pinpoint such persons before they indulge in slaughter. Such programs would conform to the thesis of those who say that 'guns do not kill people; people kill people.'

First, we must take the concrete and doable step, if we have the political and moral stamina, of making it very difficult or impossible for such murderers to obtain rapid-fire rifles – of whatever label – and magazines, clips and drums that hold dozens of bullets. Such items must be eliminated from this nation.

People will still kill, but without these guns or clips, a killer might kill two or three or four before he is taken down while reloading, or kills himself, which he commonly does. The Newtown, Connecticut shooter used high-capacity guns legally purchased by his mother.

Would she now wish that she had not been able to buy the gun that her son used to kill her and the twenty children?

Some want more guns for self-defense. Okay, so we could provide students with loaded pistols and teach them how to shoot. Or arm the teachers and train them to shoot. Then we could have the following scenario: A gunman with a semi-automatic and several high-capacity clips enters the school and starts shooting. The teachers rush to where they have guns safely locked safely away from the children. They shout to the shooter to wait until they get and load their guns to have a more fair fight.

Are lone psychopaths with military-type weapons 'a well-regulated militia?' Do the parents of the lost children believe that lone murderers are to be protected by the second amendment?

The gun that killed the children in Connecticut was not an assault rifle, according to the legal definition of assault rifles. Care to guess who writes such definitions? Did we elect some of them?

ARLAND R. MEADE

Published: the Lake Wales News 12-29-2012

Defense Is the Wrong Name

The United States Department of Defense is a misnomer. It is really the department of war, as it was when I was young many decades ago.

We spend trillions of dollars under the pretense that it is for national defense. The United States has not fought a war in defense since the one started by the Japanese against us in 1941. We have seemingly, almost eagerly, initiated or become involved in several protracted wars in other parts of the world, notably Asia, Vietnam, Korea, Iraq, Afghanistan, and in little wars such as in Granada and Haiti.

There seems to be almost no limit to what our government will appropriate, so long as it is labeled defense. Of course, we need to consider that word, but in more than a half century no nation or combination of nations has attacked the United States.

Currently in defense against these nonthreats we spend more than the next 10 other major nations of the world combined.

Has anyone noticed the effect on our national debt?

If we changed the name of Department of Defense back to the Department of War, perhaps we taxpayers would start asking ourselves whether we really need a war in Afghanistan against the al-Qaida gang, or in Iraq against the purported weapons of mass destruction, or in the civil war in Vietnam on some discredited domino theory or in Korea to keep that peninsula divided into two nations.

We need another president like Dwight Eisenhower to remind and warn us of the cost and dangers of the military-industrial complex.

ARLAND R. MEADE

Published: the Lakeland Ledger 12-18-2012

A KISS Election

The just completed election can be astoundingly revealing. Fitting it into the "Keep It Simple, Stupid" category, it went like this. The persons who people elected to the federa, chiefly, and state government, spend little on themselves. So they spent huge sums of the people's money, present and future, on the people. The people hate to have money spent on them, so they voted many of these formely chosen persons out of office.

Many shouted, "Take back our country".

Sure, take it back to when? People pressure has caused government to spend billions on services people want. You know, on "trivial" operations like Medicare, Medicaid, schools, police, interstate highways, the military – well, maybe that was done on pressure from the people.

So the people have had enough of this appropriating money for the people. Serves the people right for spending money on the people.

So let's take spending back to, for example, what we spend money for in Abraham Lincoln's days.

Is that back far enough? People should not let people spend money on people unless it is provided for in our Constitution. That seems simple enough even for the Tea Party.

ARLAND R. MEADE

Written: 11-20-2012

Which Peaceful Nation?

Sometimes I receive from a stock brokerage firm invitations to invest in specific companies or funds. Each solicitation includes a statement that past performance is no guarantee of future performance. I wonder whether such a statement should be applied to nations. Is a nation's history any indication of its future actions? Let's take Iran and the United States of America as one test comparison. Our political leaders of both major parties perpetually proclaim that Iran is a dangerous nation, a threat to us and to its neighbors. So let us compare Iran's and the U.S.' past actions and project a future based on them.

During this past decade, the United States has initiated two wars — one against a dictator in Iraq, and the other against the former ruling party in Afghanistan. Neither country had ever militarily threatened U.S. soil, and had little power to do so. During the same period, Iran invaded nobody.

During the Twentieth Century, the United States fought in two world wars. Of course there are good arguments for this, including Adolph Hitler and the Holocaust. But our soil had not been attacked by Germany when we declared war on it. About a decade later, we took sides in a Korean war and lost many thousands of Americans. About a decade after that, we took sides in a long war in Vietnam in which about fifty-eight thousand more Americans were killed. Then there was our invasion of Granada, military intervention in Haiti and Nicaragua, and perhaps others. During the same century Iran invaded no country, but did about 30 years ago fight a defensive war against Iraq, a war in which we backed Saddam Hussein's Iraq.

During the Nineteenth Century the USA had several wars, including a war against Spanish Mexico after which we annexed part of Mexico, the bitter and bloody war we fought to prevent the Southern states from having a nation of their choice, and another war against Spain after which we annexed Cuba and the Philippines for several decades. The history of the U.S. doesn't go back many more centuries, but that of Iran does. We know that when Iran was Persia, it had an empire that was stopped at Greece. For many centuries since, it has had but one notable war, the one with Iraq about 30 years ago.

Now, if I may play Devil's Advocate, to our investment analogy: If we decide that past wars are not good predictors of future wars, then we can choose the USA as a safer (more peaceful) bet than Iran. But if we think that past performance is an indication of the future, we should decide that Iran is a safer bet for peace than is the USA.

ARLAND R. MEADE

Published: the Lake Wales News 10-17-2012

No President Can Be Messiah

Humans seem to have an innate, and perhaps inescapable, need to have leaders or chiefs who will guide them and who they need, or at least want, to follow. This want to some degree counters what we think of as pure democracy.

We have observed that tyranny of the majority is possible; that some power of one or a few is necessary to protect the needs of minorities.

Examples:

• The need of slaves for an Abraham Lincoln to take (at the time) the politically unpopular step of proclaiming them free.

•The need of religious minorities for a Supreme Court to protect them from a majority-imposed religion.

People want powerful, but not all-powerful leaders. Leaders are leaders, but are not saviors. Many people imbue their leaders with supposed miraculous ability to solve their collective and even individual problems.

Does this want for extraordinary abilities and powers in a leader come to the fore in our presidential elections? Surely. Voters expect not only to choose a leader, but also expect the leader to come up with a magic wand to solve all their problems.

Do we have many millions unemployed? Just expect the president to magically give them all jobs. This expectation is nonsense, but millions act and vote as if a presidential wand can wave them to employment. No president has, or ever had, the unilateral power to do this.

Each candidate may claim to have detailed plans (kept undisclosed, of course) to accomplish economic cure. A dictator in a fascist state or a king with divine rights would come closer to having such unilateral power, but we would hate that unfettered control over our lives.

So, voters, go ahead and indulge your fantasy of the magic powers of someone you believe has the right wand. Then vote him out when that wand sputters.

ARLAND R. MEADE

Published: the Lakeland Ledger 9-17-2012

Golden Politics

My mother sometimes would say "Silence is golden."

Silence IS golden. I am pondering about golden politics. Don't laugh!

Here is the scenario I dreamed of:
A national television company announced that it would broadcast an hour-long program about Republican proposals to reduce unemployment. The program opened with the statement that each Republican proposal would be presented in detail.

Announcer:

• *The first proposal to reduce unemployment is to oppose all moves to make the wealthy pay a penny more in taxes*

• *The second proposal is to pass laws reducing or eliminating federal programs that spend money on citizens who are not wealthy.*

• *The third proposal is to refuse to cut military spending or to reduce the hundreds of military installations in scores of countries around the world.*

• *The fourth proposal is to change Medicare and Medicaid into voucher programs, which* *would increase the profits of the insurance companies at the expense of the poor and the senior citizens.*

• *The fifth proposal is to spend no Federal money to put the millions out-of-work construction workers to work repairing our crumbling roads, water mains, sewer systems, electric grids, or any other infrastructure projects.*

• *The sixth proposal is to pass a Balanced Budget Amendment.*

• *The seventh proposal is, well, we'll get to that...*

For the remaining 56 minutes of the hour there was only dead silence.

Announcer, concluding: "The previous hour was a program paid for by the Republican National Committee to elect the next President of the United States."

My dream was over. Now I knew how to vote.

ARLAND R. MEADE

Written: 9-5-2012

To Defend Against Whom?

I have always thought that the purpose of a nation's army is to defend against foreign attacking forces. Our policies on Afghanistan seems to have invented a new purpose.

The only foreign troops in Afghanistan are from the United States and NATO. the Afghan national army has more troops than these foreign forces, but has not been fighting them.

President Obama states that by 2014 the Afghan army will be strong enough to defend the nation. Against whom? Against all foreign troops?

We should have noticed that the Afghans have governed themselves. They had a national government controlled by the ultra-conservative party we label Taliban. These are native Afghans, not invaders. We, in the 1980s supported them when the Russians were the invaders. Afghanistan then was able to govern itself. They took no action against the United States.

Came September 11, 2001. A gang of Saudi Arabians known Al Qaeda, living in Afghanistan, struck the United States with American airplanes. The pilots were Saudis trained in the United States and armed with box cutting knives. No Afghans participated in the planning, financing, or execution of this attack. So when the United States invaded Afghanistan, millions of Afghans must in bewilderment have asked, "What did we do to cause this?"

Suddenly the U.S. declared that the Afghans could not govern themselves. Now our President says that they will be able to defend themselves by 2014. There's the matter of Al Qaeda. Of course we should have gone after Al Qaeda's leaders, but to invade a nation?

The Al Qaeda gang happened to be in Afghanistan, but the 9-11 attack could have been conceived and planned from Saudi Arabia, Rome, Chicago, or anywhere. If they had been in Rome, would we have invaded all of Italy until we were convinced that the Italians could govern themselves?

Poor Afghanistan! It is time to declare that the Afghan people are capable of governing themselves, and that their national army is strong enough to defend their nation.

ARLAND R. MEADE

Written: 7-7-2012

Allowing Is Not Favoring

In a simple-minded attempt to simplify the news, our attractive and glib TV anchors and newscasters enunciate some flat out lies. For example, I have heard several say several times that President Obama has announced that he is "in favor of same sex marriage". This is plainly false.

Imagine this: At pillow talk some night the President states to his wife, "I am in favor of same sex marriage". We can feel the bedroom suddenly become cooler.

For years President Obama has stated that he believes that marriage between a man and a woman is culturally and religiously the norm.

The over-paid voices of the broadcast media are experts at non-stop talking without pausing for punctuation, breath, or thought. Their interpretations are more vital to them than the facts. When the President stated that he believed that couples of the same sex should be "allowed to marry and have the same legal status as others", he did not say he favored same sex marriage. He merely asserted that it should not be legally forbidden.

Often we may forgive for sloppy use of our language, but the influential broadcast personalities should be taken to the woodshed for such blatant misstatements.

ARLAND R. MEADE

Written 5-12-2012

The Wars and the Yuan

Our government leaders discuss and debate how to get out of the two forged wars in Asia. Here is one that would be quick and I have not heard it mentioned.

The wars were initiated without providing to pay for them by increasing taxes. That would have been the honorable, and fiscally responsible way. So the costs are covered by selling US bonds, primarily to China. That increases our national debt by that much – more actually.

China is hinting that they may not value such bonds for long. So if China would stop buying them, our Congress would immediately have to initiate tax increases to pay for the wars.

Inasmuch as the Republicans are adamant against tax increases, even though they started the wars, they would be in a dilemma; either raise taxes or declare that we have won and bring our troops and vast equipment home.

As we probably have no use for many war tanks, etc. we would leave them anyway. That happens after wars.

And finally our nation would be following the principle of pay up or shut up.

ARLAND R. MEADE

Written: 5-9-2012

Oil Sands 'Creation'

In this political season we expect to hear pronouncements that do not square with the facts. But an oil industry commercial aired frequently tops them all for absurdity.

The spokesman indicated that if there would be no governmental interference, the industry 'would be able to produce oil sands.'

We know from reliable sources that Canada already has huge quantities of oil sands. The oil interests claim powers that I assume belong to God – or to Mother Nature – that is, to produce, that is create, the sands from which man can extract oil.

The industry can extract oil from the sands, but it cannot produce the sands. How can a multi-billion dollar industry make such an inconceivably silly misstatement?

How much should that affect out trust in its other statements?

It would be more appropriate to thank the Power that the oil sand's there in the first place.

ARLAND R. MEADE

Published: the Lake Wales News 4-21-2012

Why Do We Call Them Allies?

Often our governmental leaders and others speak of "the allies of the United States." Typically, these are referred to as helpful to us, even necessary.

I suggest that such claims are mostly pipe dreams, fiction. Egypt was one of our allies to which we contributed billions to build and maintain its military, to defend against what enemies? For years we speak of our ally Pakistan, to which we give billions for its military without identifying which nations might attack it. India, maybe? India is another of our alleged allies.

To which ally should we give the most money? The ally most in the news is Israel. Recently it was announced that we were granting Israel $3 billion for its military, for its defense – or perhaps for offense.

For sure, one requirement for any nation to be an ally of the United States is that it ac- cepts billions of our dollars for its military establishment.

If we were to be attacked, would Pakistan, Egypt, Israel and other so-called allies leap to defend us? How? Such happenings would be the theme of cartoons.

I suggest that our allies cost us too much. Call them partial dependents, not allies. This is especially conspicuous with Israel. That nation is our dependent. The cost to us has been billions, and our participation in another Middle East war could be added to those billions.

So, let's give billions if we see fit, but let's not pretend that this is because Israel, or any of the aforementioned countries, is our ally.

ARLAND R. MEADE

Published: the Lakeland Ledger 3-23-2012

Supreme Court vs. God

Is a corporation a person? The U.S. Supreme Court ruled that it is. This is a tremendous matter, as is shown in part by the birth of the unrestricted and not accountable donations by corporations to political action committees.

It is almost universally believed that God created humans, which we also label 'people' (persons). The words in the Christian Bible state this, and it is the same in other religions.

After uncountable years, persons created corporations. No contradiction there. I state it this way: God created humans, that is, persons, and persons created corporations, which are not persons. Corporations are therefore not persons, no matter what the Supreme Court ruled. Therefore, corporations should not have the rights of individual persons.

ARLAND R. MEADE

Published: the Polk County Democrat 2-18-2012

Chinese vs. U.S. Factories

A participant on a recent TV panel explained that China was able to employ multimillions of factory workers because the Chinese government spent billions of dollars to build new factories. He suggested that the United States could do the same. Of course he did not explain how this could be done.

Let's follow the money. I presume that the government does not get these billions from under the pillow, from a fairy godmother. I presume that the U.S. government would try to borrow it from China or from taxes. Now possibly the Chinese would balk at this if they knew that it would be used to subsidize new factories to compete with Chinese ones. If the Chinese became unwilling to continue lending the U.S. money, the U.S. government could not go deeper into debt even if it tried to.

Absent money borrowed from China, the government would be required to increase taxes on Americans. Our taxpayers are told, or learn, that the billions or trillions of added taxes are to subsidize new factories so that the United States could undercut the effect of China doing the same thing. Can you hear the politicians' roar of "no new taxes?"

The Chinese may find it necessary to pay more taxes to enable their nation to industrialize faster. Americans are less likely to accept higher taxes to make it possible for American workers to compete on an even field with Chinese workers. Want to bet?

ARLAND R. MEADE

Published: the Lakeland Ledger 2-14-2012

No More Nines

Say no to nine. I do not mean the 9-9-9 proposal of presidential candidate Herman Cain. I refer to the foolish pricing of almost every item marketed from store shelves or advertised in billions of newspapers, direct mail pieces, on broadcast channels and over the Internet.

The nines are almost universal. Is this economic or psychological? You know, $9.99, $19.99, $29.99, $99.99, $199.99 and others. I have seen a diamond ring advertised as "Only $499.99." I wonder whether the lover who bought this would have bought it if it had been advertised at $500. Would his sweetheart be pleased that he saved a penny? Or that a lady would shun such a cheap jewel, wanting to have the one that cost a penny more.

I have even seen a fur coat advertised for $999. Do you suppose that we thrifty consumers would not buy a $1,000 fur coat, but would buy one for a dollar less?

Who is being ridiculous with these nines? Do the merchants know, or believe, that their goods will not sell without taking a penny or a dollar off a reasonable price? Or is the American public so frugal, or silly, as to base its purchase on a penny per item.

In the days of Ben Franklin, probably, a penny saved was a penny earned. He did state that.

With today's value of money, is the use of tons of paper, and hours of time on broadcasts, to state all these nines sensible or even meaningful? Or are all these nines a sign of American decadence?

I suggest that we start saying no to nine.

ARLAND R. MEADE

Published: the Lakeland Ledger 1-30-2012

Repetitive Redundancies

Maybe TV and radio commentators and newscasters believe in excessive redundancy, or maybe they do not listen to what they have said.

Recently a radio professional stated that something would be postponed "until later." Did he presume that we might think that something could be postponed until earlier?

More than once I have heard a TV anchor state that he, or she, was about to include part of an interview with a famous person "before that person died." Perhaps he wanted to make sure that we would not assume the interview was not made after the person had died.

And how often have you heard that something will happen "in the future."

Why do professional communicators hedge on a figure impossible to be doubted? A book reviewer for a new book stated that every day President Barack Obama receives 12,000 letters and emails. He went on with the statement that the president "might" not read every one, but ... Would any of us believe that he could?

Fortunately, we can often read into a faulty statement what the person means. Here are examples: "General Electric pays less income tax than a plumber". "Warren Buffet pays less income tax than does his secretary". These speakers meant that GE and Buffet pay a lower rate. Is it too much to expect these million dollar broadcasters to be accurate?

When our elected representatives write laws, they will, I hope, pay more attention to our language than do the million-dollar radio and TV personalities.

Now what I write and say will influence few. Some will respond with the typical phrase: "I could care less." They mean, of course, that they could not care less.

But what does a fuddy-duddy 96-year-old know about how people should communicate?

ARLAND R. MEADE

Published: the Lakeland Ledger 1-2-2012

Education Not the Solution

Some Americans tout more education as a way to significantly reduce unemployment in the United States.

Did thousands of our factories close and millions of jobs disappear because we lacked education? Of course not; these jobs went to Asia because workers were abundant there at far lower cost. Are workers on Chinese assembly lines more educated than millions of Americans who lost such jobs?

Business is business, and many propose that our government be run more like a business. Not so fast! This could lead to yet more outsourcing. Would you like to see a million Asians join our military forces at half the dollars paid to Americans?

To dramatize my point, let us presume that a genie waves a magic wand and instantly all our high school and college students have graduated, including those studying for advanced degrees. Do you see U.S. business leaders rushing to reopen assembly lines so these millions of better-educated people can step forward to make items the Asians are currently making for us? Or would you see these Americans added to the unemployed? Can you hear them begging the government to do something to create more jobs? Another magic wand is needed.

To believe that education will cure our unemployment woes, is, to use an old expression, hogwash. In as much as I possess three college degrees, I should use a more erudite term. How about 'porcine grime removing shampoo?'

Of course more education is favorable to most people and nations, but to proclaim that it can do much to reduce our current unemployment is, well, just hogwash.

ARLAND R. MEADE

Published: Polk County Democrat 12-31-2011

Regression toward the Mean of One-Worldism Cannot Be Stopped

Call it one-worldism. Some call the trend in economics globalization. They discuss the problems in terms of economics, recession, finance, unemployment, free trade, regulation and more.

To most of us, the focus must be on unemployment and on why wages for most are moving downward in the United States.

More than a half century ago, Wendell Wilkie, Republican nominee for president of the United States, wrote and talked about one world. He did not get elected, and we do not hear much about one world.

One world we will never live to see, but the direction toward it is unstoppable. No matter what our government does or which party wins, nor who promises, the United States will never return to the glory days of high wages and economic dominance. Nor will China or any other nation reach the position once reached by the United States.

General Motors may survive one-world competition by rehiring workers at half the rate they would have received a few years ago. The same applies to workers in other closed or almost-closed manufacturing enterprises.

The wherewithal of different parts of the globe will prevent wages from becoming the same the world over, but the wages of richer nations will continue to trend downward while wages of other nations will trend upward. Both move toward the mean.

You can ignore the promises of economists and politicians in any nation. Our regression toward the mean will happen. We hope that some of the most rich individuals can be made to help the workers.

I am 96 years old and one-worldism has little time to affect me. I am concerned for those half or a quarter my age. Sorry, guys.

ARLAND R. MEADE

Published: the Lakeland Ledger 10-13-2011

Replacing Medicare

During the many, many hours of arguments over replacing Medicare with the Republican privatization plan (with massive federal subsidies to the insurance companies), I have heard not a word about the added entertainment factors of the Republican plan. For example, consider how much we would enjoy the deluge of ads on television from the multitudes of insurance companies, each wanting a profitable piece of the new health pie.

We already have a taste of what would come, in the ads now inundating us with insurance plans to supplement Medicare.

How much we would enjoy the additional commercials on TV, radio, and online.

Imagine the delight we will get each day to find our mailboxes stuffed with brochures soliciting insurance business from us. Great to relax in an easy chair and peruse them.

Also consider the pleasure that publishers will have in providing us with pages of commercials to read for policies to replace the deceased Medicare, and our satisfaction in new employment generated for copywriters, artists, layout specialists and so on. We enjoy creating jobs, don't we?

Built into the insurance policy rates are, of course, the costs of providing all these entertainments, not to mention paying the stockholders and ¬multimillion-dollar compensation packages to the top executives.

We, unhappily of course, avoid all this with the one-payer Medicare and Medicaid systems, as well as the government programs' low administrative costs and comprehensive coverage.

You note that I am not taking political sides; I simply want to point out the goodies we will not get if we keep Medicare.

ARLAND R. MEADE

Published: the Lakeland Ledger 5-12-2011

Lincoln Killed His Own People Too

Political leaders, and others, are currently condemning the head of government of Libya for 'killing his own people."

Of course he is, but that is normal when rebellions occur and it itself does not put him into history as an evil person, although we presume that he is that.

By that metric we would label our famous president Abraham Lincoln as evil.

Throughout history when a position of the citizens of any nation revolt against their government, their government fights back and people are killed. Which side is right or wrong about any issues does not change that fact.

Did King George kill any residents of his nation — The American colonies were part of his nation then — and vice versa? Of course.

Possibly no leader in history led the fighting that caused the death of more of the rebels, the other side, than did Abraham Lincoln. Do we condemn him for this? Some do, and I am one of them.

No one proclaimed, it appears, that he was killing many thousands of his own people, the southerners, people who were his own, at least until they rebelled. The North called them rebels, and his decisions caused many thousands of his own side to die.

Read the statistics, or watch the Ken Burns' film about the Civil War, on public television. This was America's bloodiest and meanest war.

So feel free to hate Gaddafi for whatever evil deeds he has committed, but don't be so sloppy in use of terms such as "killing his own people" unless you are willing to use the same words for President Lincoln.

ARLAND R. MEADE

Published: Fort Meade Leader 4-13-2011

Cycle of Borrowing

Our economists and government spokesmen have told us, repeatedly, that our economic breakdown of 2008 was caused by the massive amount of debt: houses we could not pay for, government spending beyond its income and more.

This seems rational and simple.

Now they are begging us to spend more, and especially to borrow more.

They complain that banks are not lending enough to businesses and others.

Surely more lending would create more debt.

The theme is that we will recover economically by doing exactly what got us into the trouble in the first place.

I'm reminded of the political slogan in a previous decade - KISS - "Keep It Simple, Stupid."

Our elected officials are now keeping it simple. But the unspoken emphasis is on the word "stupid."

I wonder who is being the most stupid.

ARLAND R. MEADE

Published: the Lakeland Ledger 1-14-2011

It Isn't Over Until It Is Over

Our economists should change their definition of "recession" and of "over."

For a few months they have stated that the recession is over.

Millions unemployed Americans and others are not fooled. A sad aspect is that some journalists parrot the economists without a critique.

Let's convert this situation into a fable.

Once upon a time a great nation had a shock in the financial operations, and millions of persons became unemployed.

The number got greater and greater during a couple of years. Then the gross national product increased a trifle. Economists promptly announced that the recession was over. They did this even though millions were still unemployed and businesses had cut back or even closed.

The citizens knew that, for example, when a door is opened it is not closed while it is still open, and that a person is not out of a well while he is still at the bottom, and that the recession is not over while it is at its worst point.

So they seized the most famous economists and devised a demonstration to teach them about recessions, and to prove that a recession is not over until it is over.

They dubbed this "underwater economics." They built a submersible. Into this they put the economists.

They then submerged it in the Potomac River nine feet. The economists were informed that this represented the depth of the recession which was close to its worst point.

When the recession grew less, the people raised the submersible one foot for each million persons who became employed. Eventually, the nation returned to about what it was when the recession started.

That signaled that the recession was finally over. The economists were freed and they confessed that they had been wrong and they revised their method of predicting. They promised never again to pretend that something was over until it was over.

And the entire nation rejoiced and both political parties shook hands across the aisle and went to work fixing the problems of the nation.

ARLAND R. MEADE

Published: the Lake Wales News 12-1-2010

Pay-As-You-Go Politics

Americans believe in and live on the pay-as-you-go principle. The just-completed election demonstrates that. Americans hate indulging themselves now and paying later. And they hold their legislators, especially those in our federal government, to this principle.

We voters discovered that our legislators appropriated money for certain people, especially the elderly and sick ones, without establishing income provisions, that is, taxes, to pay for them. You know, programs such as Social Security, Medicare, Medicaid, education, a highway system, CIA, FBI, police, new bridges, a few earmarks, a couple of wars and more. Those legislators thought the public wanted these activities and would pay later. How simple-minded, how American!

So the people rose up, many shouting "throw the rascals out and take back our government." Now those rascals, for various reasons, including ego and wish to help their nation, worked hard to get elected to these not-for-profit positions. Federal legislators cannot in our democracy pay themselves very much. For that they should become CEO of a health-insurance company.

So they try to please their constituents and appropriate money in excess of taxes received. This puts our budget into the red and invites the Chinese to buy U.S. bonds. We expect to pay later, as we would when we buy a car on credit or a house on which there is a mortgage.

So when these not-for-profit legislators tried to help people without making the people pay as they go, the people voted them out of office. Serves them right.

Do the voters get what they want or what they deserve?

ARLAND R. MEADE

Published: the Lakeland Ledger 11-16-2010

Need a Smaller Government

Millions of voters are clamoring against big government, high taxes, and too much debt - not their own mind you, but government debt cause by those horrible aliens called politicians.

To rectify all of these conditions we first must change our vocabulary. We need new terms so we can act sagely.

We all understand buying goods and services from those who can provide them, and that someone pays.

So we henceforth will refer to taxes as prices for goods and services we buy from the supplier and the supplier is the government.

There are no alternates to the government for certain services, such as invading Asian nations, social security, and universal health care. So we buy these items from government or we don't have them. Our choice.

A vendor can try to sell us goods or services by advertising or other means, but we, the public, are not obliged to buy. Examples:

Medicare is proposed at the cost of $xxx. We decline to buy, thereby not adding to the size of government.

Social Security is proposed, and we decline to buy, again keeping government from growing. A war in Asia is proposed at about a trillion dollars for ten years. We decline to buy.

We don't operate national parks, or the merchant marine, or the FBI or inspectors of meat and other foods, or maintain federal highways, and so on and on. We discover that the writers of our Constitution did not attend tax supported schools, so we know that such schools are not necessary.

We all can add ways not to spend money, keep so called taxes low, and avoid big government.

We the people can buy or not buy suggested actions and services.

A democracy can choose the kind of nation it wants to be. And if our purchasing agents, aka elected officials, force services upon us, we can vote them out.

I prefer a quicker way to recall them, but for that we must alter our Constitution. Has anyone published the book "Smaller Government for Dummies?"

ARLAND R. MEADE

Published: the Polk County Democrat 9-29-2010

Tell Hows of Oil Disaster

Picture this: thousands of people cleaning the beaches of our Gulf States. For weeks, newspapers are telling us that this is happening. It is news and it is important to us.

But one of the basic six Ws of news writing is being neglected, even by the excellent Ledger, which I have appreciated since moving to Bartow from Connecticut in 1995. The how is often neglected. Perhaps because the W is at the wrong end of the word. The others are what, who, why, where, when.

This fact hit me, again, with a brief mention that someone had been cited for disposing of some of the tar balls and crude oil improperly. Where does a worker take a bucket or a truckload of tar balls to dispose of them correctly? Not in my backyard, of course.

I hope there are specialized publications that tell us the hows, but I am almost blind and cannot peruse them in a library. In fact, I no longer can read The Ledger. I'm fortunate in having a wife who daily reads the editorial page and selected articles. For me, she would not miss a how article.

The hows are not the main purpose of a daily paper, but perhaps the admirable Ledger could now and then have a next-step feature that would tell us about how tar balls are picked up, hauled and disposed of, whether salvaged by British Petroleum or others.

ARLAND R. MEADE

Published: the Lakeland Ledger, 7-11-2010

A Selfishness Poll for Health Care

In democratic United States many organizations as well as political parties take polls. Currently these are numerous in relationship to our national health and medical insurance. But I have yet to see what we might label the selfishness poll, or, to be a little more kind, a self-interest poll.

Because most senior citizens seem fearful that some new governmental law might include reducing Medicare coverage in order to give insurance to others, the poll could be simply "If you were to vote today on the following two alternatives, which would you choose?"

A. Continue the socialized medicine plan we label Medicare and let it be part of the increase in our national debt, or

B. Eliminate all Medicare coverage and reduce the national debt a bit.

Now, of course, Medicare coverage affects more than seniors, but this poll would be only taken on those on Medicare.

Do you suppose the majority would vote to give up Medicare to relieve the national debt? Would the self-interest factor be more important to senior citizens than their opinions about single payer, that is, the U.S. Treasury, we should shun?

ARLAND R. MEADE

Published: the Polk County Democrat 3-6-2010

A Simple 'Yes'

Changes in language are never-ending, and there is nothing an individual can do to get in the way of changes that grate like fingernails on a chalkboard. I am grateful that these substitutes for the simple "yes" are not much used in print media.

It has been a long time since I have heard a TV anchor or reporter or a person being interviewed on television use the word "yes," the standard affirmative word.

Instead we hear sounds that could be written as "yayah," "yehuh," "yayr," "yeha", and so on.

I've noticed these substitutes for yes for a long time, so I was pleasantly jolted into writing this letter when I heard a famous economist answer a question by simply saying "yes". I presume that if a newspaper feels obliged to quote some of these TV anchor persons, it might write "yayuh."

Perhaps these usages are generational. Perhaps the yayuh generation will be followed by one that will rediscover the affirmative "yes".

ARLAND R. MEADE

Published: the Lakeland Ledger 3-5-2010

Samaritans vs Pharisees on Health Care

Among the ways to look at our national health problem is to compare some of today's attitudes with those of the people in the time of Jesus as related in the Bible.

Some Americans, often called Democrats or liberals, lean toward the actions of the Good Samaritan, and therefore are inclined to help those less fortunate with, for example, public supported health insurance. Other Americans, often called Republicans or conservatives, act more like Pharisees, and are determined to maintain the status quo. They expect everyone to pay for their own health care, or simply suffer the consequences if they are not able to do so. And especially the Pharisee types are opposed to paying taxes to help the less fortunate.

Of course some Americans will object to these Biblical or modern labels. Labels are less important than actions and attitudes anyway. Presuming that both sides should act bipartisanly is a waste of time. I wonder whether residents of Jerusalem during Jesus' last days could have acted in a bipartisan manner and thereby kept Jesus off the cross. One side has to win.

We can be sure that in our days those who would give up a little to be one's brothers' keeper and those who would not do so can neutralize each other. Witness our Congress. I am glad that the side most Jesus-like, most Samaritan-like won in the United States Congress re the health bill battle – flawed though it is.

ARLAND R. MEADE

Written: 2-9-2010

Understanding the Taliban

Some statistics about the war in Afghanistan lead to curiosity of what is not revealed by the numbers.

A few days after President Obama's announcement that we were to send 30,000 more troops to Afghanistan, I heard one of the top four military officials in the United States say that there may be as many as 27,000 Afghan Taliban fighters.

Against them are an estimated 170,000 in the Afghan national army. Helping them, or perhaps vice versa, are at present some 60,000 American troops with airplanes, armored vehicles, drones with bombs, helicopters, etc., and thousands of service contractors.

The quantity of those items possessed by the Taliban is presumably almost nil. And then we toss in some 15,000 troops from other Western nations.

Therefore, the Taliban have numerical odds against them of at least 250,000 to 27,000. And we are told that we will train the Afghan army to be bigger and better.

Are we going to teach them to march in step? There are rumors that typically Afghan men are adept with weapons, including automatic rifles.

What is behind these numbers and why are we told that the Taliban side is gaining strength against those odds? Is it sociology, or patriotism, or religion? Do a majority of the 25 million inhabitants of Afghanistan resent foreign soldiers and the government which they support?

Do so many inhabitants support the Taliban that their side can and will carry on the fight for years or decades?

A desire not to be controlled by foreigners, especially of a different religion, is understandable, is it not? How would we feel in their situation?

We are a rich nation and we can afford to spend hundreds of billions of dollars to find the answer.

ARLAND R. MEADE

Published: Polk County Democrat 12-20-2009

Only in America

Picture this, an "Only in America" scenario. In Centerville live two children and their parents. They are good citizens with low income and low income potential. The thirty five year old mother has not been feeling well for some time, but avoided seeking medical help because they had no health insurance or enough dollars.

Finally the mother saw a doctor and was told that she had cancer, a rapidly growing type, throughout her body that might not be stoppable at such a late detection.

"Why did you delay so long?", asked the physician. We know the response. The two children were soon left motherless, because of too little, too late.

But there's a "success" part of the scenario. The dead mother has a ninety year old grandfather who has many illnesses, from which he is unlikely to recover. But he sees any physician or specialist as often as he choses. His frequent hospital stays include many tests, studies, and tubes. The bills go to Medicare, even though his doctors, family, and he himself knows he will soon die.

This happens because he is enrolled in a single-payer government directed plan called MEDICARE. He has only a few weeks, or at most a few months to live in misery. More than a hundred thousand dollars have been spent on him, because, you see, he is covered by a single-payer government plan supported by the taxpayers.

A LOOK BACK. A young mother who asks only to rear her children to be good citizens dies because her country ignores her and instead pours treasure into a dying old man. What a ghastly government and social system priority. Could this tragic inequality be tolerated in a civilized nation?

About half the national legislators and about half the population of the United States are opposed to correcting this cruel unfairness. And some stridently so.

We can be proud, or ashamed of our health care system. As the saying goes, "ONLY IN AMERICA".

I'm not wholly against using tax money to ease the final months of the old and useless guys. I note that two months ago I passed my ninety fourth birthday.

ARLAND R. MEADE

Written: 12-17-2009

The Taliban Are Afghanistan Citizens

Typically our TV newscasters, including the famous anchors, are careless or shallow in their words. For example, they typically say X number of the Taliban, often called insurgents, and XY Afghans and Americans were killed.

One hears this phrasing so often that I presume that many Americans think that the Taliban are not Afghanistan citizens. Of course, Afghans are killing Afghans.

Why are our news people not being accurate and stating, for example, that Afghan national soldiers killed XY Taliban citizens? Or that U.S. forces killed six Afghans while losing only one American. This then correctly indicates that there is a civil war going on in Afghanistan and that we are taking sides. That hardly will endear us to the population of the country, no matter which side we take.

Now most Americans don't favor governments controlled by religious fanatics or extremists, which the Taliban fighters are. We have had our own experience.

For example, the Puritans of Massachusetts in the 17th Century. Many individuals who violated what the religious leaders said that God wanted were condemned by the official government, which was controlled by the church. This led to the hanging of 20 innocent persons in Salem during 1692 because the government was controlled by the Puritan beliefs about witchcraft. Five years later, Salem had a fast day and declared that the persons were improperly convicted. A plea for atonement, but that did not help the dead.

Regardless of the awfulness of Taliban beliefs, the citizens we call the Taliban are Afghans. Furthermore, not a one of them participated in the Al Qaeda attacks on Sept. 11, 2001, nor did they ever threaten the U.S. when they were the national government. That was after they led the battles over 10 years that forced the Russians to pull out. The Russians lost about 10,000 troops in 10 years.

It is always difficult to eliminate a radical religious people and no matter how many years we fight in Afghanistan, we will not be able to kill all or even most of the Taliban.

Why do some Americans think it is smart to try to accomplish the impossible? Are we inhaling too much of the product of Afghan poppies? After all, America is the major market for that product.

ARLAND R. MEADE

Published: the Polk County Democrat 10-7-2009

Let Afghans Choose Future

In 1776 King George had a low regard for the people in the colonies who revolted against his government rules. They were contemptuously called rebels. We in America call them patriots.

In Afghanistan we are losing troops and money fighting groups we call rebels. I don't know what the Afghans call them, but history may call them patriots. We think it strange that those who we call the Taliban (which means students) are fighting against our invading troops. Perhaps they resent foreign troops in their country – even peace-loving Americans.

Our government and press seem to have ignored the fact that no members of the Taliban were involved in the flying of our airliners into towers. Nor has the Afghan government threatened the United States. It did tolerate the Arabic Al Qaida inside the borders. Those guys are now apparently in Pakistan, and other parts of the world, but we insist on bombing in Afghanistan rather than in those nations.

Some of those Taliban who fought against the American invaders are our guests at Guantanamo.

Some have died there. Those we captured fighting our invading troops should be sent home. And we should start saving money and lives by bringing our military home.

We don't have to approve of the Taliban social positions. They are very un-American. For example, they forbid drinking of alcohol, but tolerate stoning of women (not men) for adultery. To us the Taliban are religious fanatics. They and we proclaim "God is good." On that we may agree, but God's children of both faiths can really mess up human relations.

I'm for letting the Afghan decide for themselves whether their Taliban or our troops are their patriots.

ARLAND R. MEADE

Published: the Lakeland Ledger, 9-26-2009

Words and Cowards

Americans in public positions are afraid of speaking the truth, and those in high positions are the most afraid – downright cowardly sometimes.

An example, Bernanke, director of the Federal Reserve, this week said that the recession is very likely over. This is of course a direct lie in the use of the word "over". Millions of unemployed know that. We know that the loss of jobs has slowed, that some prices in the stock markets are edging upward. And that there is evidence that some or much of the tax money appropriated to solve the economic crash is not likely to be paid back.

Is this the end of the recession, as some state, or the depression, as some claim; or evidence that the recessions is "over"? Nonsense.

What may be the fact is that we have reached the bottom, or worst point of the recession. That we are fully into, that this is as bad as it will get. Being that bad is not being over – the depression – it is just the point when we might start a recovery. We fare at the bottom of the pit and expect improvement. Being at the worst point, the bottom, is not being "over", the recession.

Being at the economic point where we will not go lower is like being at the bottom of a well and noticing that we can't fall further. That may be good news, but to declare that we are out of the well, that our depression is over is just a plain false use of words, and lying foolishly.

Perhaps our great leaders know that we would revolt at the truth, so they are politically smart to lie to us. Maybe so, and maybe so, and we ought to be ashamed of ourselves as well as of them.

ARLAND R. MEADE

Written: 9-20-2009

44

"Affordable" AKA "Someone Else Pays"

Prominent among the avalanche of words dumped on us by our political leaders and economists is the word "affordable". As used in the discussions about health care, this simply means that health care for individuals is affordable according to how much other people pay for it.

I have no objection to the President and members of Congress having affordable health insurance, meaning paid for from the Federal Treasury. Their mind should be free of such personal problems so that they can spend time on governing.

Now let's get down the line on being affordable.

Most government workers at many levels have their insurance policies subsidized by tax money, thereby making it affordable for most of them. Millions who have good jobs with major companies have health insurance subsidized by the employers making it affordable for them.

Millions of low income workers have no one to subsidize health insurance policies, so they typically have no health insurance as they cannot afford the policies. This, of course, also applies to the millions of unemployed, the already sick, and others.

So, any position on insurance for everybody, whether called public or commercial is nonsense unless the first consideration is WHO PAYS? And we are not hearing that. Instead we just get vagueness and nonsense with the weasel word "affordable".

Until Americans are willing to conclude that the providing health insurance for our poorest millions is both humane and in the long run the most beneficial, we'll continue our American hodgepodge. Millions will have "affordable" aka subsidized health insurance, while millions of the poorest will have no subsidy and still no health insurance.

ARLAND R. MEADE

Written: 9-15-2009

Health Co-op Won't Work

Some of our national figures glibly suggest cooperatives to take the place of what is labeled the public option health care insurance proposal.

Members of cooperatives pay their way for all operations, goods and services. Sometimes they save a little money.

But health cooperatives would do nothing whatever to provide health care for the poor and unemployed and others who cannot pay out of pocket for commercial health insurance.

Cooperatives can do nothing whatever to solve the problem for about 50 million Americans. Nothing whatever.

I'm not just being theoretical. For some years of my professional life, I was on the headquarters staff of a nine-state agricultural cooperative. Farm supplies and services are, of course, not health services, but a cooperative is a cooperative, and members must pay for everything they receive.

Nothing wrong with that, but cooperatives have no magic. Someone must pay the total load. To claim that cooperatives are any kind of solution for the millions of Americans not insured is simply being ignorant or pulling the uninsured wool over our eyes.

I have yet to see any proposal for public insurance policies that would provide health care for about 50 million uninsured.

Only a complete replacement of our commercial insurance system by a single payer plan something like Canada's can accomplish that. Anything else is a pipe dream, or a pipe nightmare.

ARLAND R. MEADE

Published: the Polk County Democrat 9-12-2009

46

Universal One-Payer Federal System

The American public is being buried in words about health care, but the words bring extremely few facts. We expect the political leaders we choose to be vague, but much of the verbiage provides generalities and objectives but next to nothing about means and procedures.

And the TV and press presenters either don't dig for facts or there are not any to be found. How about straightforward answers to the following?

If we establish a "public option" insurance for the 47 million or so uninsured residents, do those millions pay specific shares of the cost and how much? Or will the entire cost be charged to the taxpayers as is Medicare today?

If most of the uninsured residents are that way because they cannot afford the premiums, what option can be given to them other than free — that is — taxpayer paid premiums? If there is no premium cost for the public option, what would prevent everyone on the present insurance managed healthcare plans from immediately signing up for the "free" plan?

If Company A has a plan with required premiums, of say, $10,000 per year, and Company B has a plan for $8,800, some may elect to buy the higher price one because of some preferred details. This is normal business. If there is an added public option, how many of the poor would buy it at any price except free? Same question for the unemployed and ill. So a public option is impossible unless it is fully or almost fully paid for from the federal treasury. This kind of public/private mix will force a complete collapse of the concept of insuring everyone.

A universal one-payer federal system such as most of the industrialized nations have is the only possible way for universal coverage. Costly? Of course. But even the cost proclaimed by Republicans is about the same as we spend fighting two wars in Asia.

We might not have that many nations who can afford universal health care but cannot afford to invade other nations as we, the United States of America, can and did. But we are the leaders of the world, so of course our priorities are correct.

I have realized, of course, that we might decide to cease foreign wars some time, although it would be almost impossible to terminate a single-payer public insurance plan. But a single-payer public plan would be good for us.

ARLAND R. MEADE

Published: the Polk County Democrat 8-26-2009

Learning a Foreign Language

Recently I read a long, informative article about the major cutbacks in foreign language teaching in our schools – largely because of money shortages. This may be a bad thing, but it could lead to something better.

I've been a senior citizen for many years. I studied French in high school and have traveled a little abroad. So did millions of others through the decades.

Now, how many of us ever found any practical use of what we learned? We either never traveled to the nations where the language we studied was spoken, or if we did, we mostly found that what we learned was not enough to make much difference. Or we traveled with tour groups and the language problems were taken care of for us.

Learning a foreign language, especially when we are very young, probably help develop our brains. At least we are told that. And certainly the second language requires some learning of grammar that we could fumble through without knowing as we go through the American school system. Better understanding of grammar we should find useful, even if we never leave our home town. Or especially. The study of Latin has value in that, although Latin has not been a language of any nation for centuries.

There exists a way our children could get the benefits of brain stretching and more understanding of grammar in a very, very low cost and easy way: a year studying the international constructed language Esperanto. Any willing public school teacher can conduct such learning. Believe me.

Esperanto is wholly regular in grammar, spelling, and word stress. Being designed for function rather than for fatherland, the language requires one to understand what grammar is and how meaningful words are built and altered. I believe that in one semester of Esperanto students would inevitably learn more about how grammar and words function than they learn in several years of instruction in English and/or through the irregularities and idiosyncrasies of any national language.

ARLAND R. MEADE

Written: 6-11-2009

Solve Crisis By Repetition?

After viewing and listening to dozens of political and financial leaders talk via radio and television and reading newspapers, I presume that the financial crisis was caused by excessive borrowing, partly to live beyond our incomes or to live the American dream – with an excess of confidence pushed along by eager and sometimes fraudulent lenders. Now we are told by these same distinguished characters that the way out is to create more borrowing – also called more credit – and develop more confidence.

Although we got into the trouble while having an abundance of confidence, and a lot of big and easy credit flow, we are being told that to get out of the crises we must do a lot of exactly what got us into the calamity.

I'm reminded of what some prescribe to alleviate an alcoholic hangover. It's called hair of the dog. So we are urged to cure the financial debacle by a hair-of-the-dog treatment.

For those of us who doubt that this logic is logical, I hope that some investigative reporter will present a clarification.

ARLAND R. MEADE

Published: The Lakeland Ledger 4-1-2009

What a Waste

Very recently I experienced a hospital stay. The operation was successful, or probably I would not be alive to write this. I'm grateful. The result extends, for years perhaps, the life of a man of 93 years who can never again lay a brick, hammer a nail, or otherwise produce any tangible value to society. And the expense was many thousands of dollars. What a waste!

The costs of the procedures were covered by the single payer health plan called Medicare. Like any other taxpayer, I have paid toward this socialized medicine program made law over four decades ago by misguided liberals in government. Think of the money we taxpayers could have saved if we had no such socialized medicine for seniors!

I know that Medicare and Medicaid are not in the popular mind "socialized medicine", but of course they are. So I cogitated on how much we could cut taxes if all medical care were entirely privatized and put exclusively into the hands of the insurance companies and "health maintenance organizations" (HMOs).

But why stop at putting only medical care into private hands? Why not also privatize other necessary community services such as emergency medical services, police, schools, fire departments, and sanitation services? Then we would not pay taxes for those functions. I'm sure that entrepreneurs would rapidly form corporations to solicit membership for policing, firefighting, educating, etc.

Over many decades we could enjoy being inundated with junk mail solicitations and TV advertising by companies vying for business. But I'd enjoy all this, as I'd be one of those people with principled objections against socializing such functions.

Let's visualize a scenario I likely would have befallen a month ago had we taxpayers not been so foolish as to vote for the liberals who in 1965 ushered in Medicare (aka socialized medicine for the elderly). There of course would have been from the '60s on, competing corporations begging me to buy medical care insurance through them. So I pick a company that is large, well reputed, and guaranteed by American International Insurance Group (AIG). I duly pay the rates imposed by the insurance company or HMO. What could go wrong?

Now in 2009 I require costly medical care, as I in fact did a month ago. The providing insurance company, having invested in mortgage backed securities, is now bankrupt, but there is that giant AIG to back it. Oops, AIG too, is billions in the hole, so my medical bills might not get paid and the cost-conscious hospital might scrimp on or deny treatment. Or, horror of horrors, the medical insurance company and its trusty backstop AIG would get bailed out by the American taxpayer.

I recover, the taxpayer puts up the money, and the CEOs of the medical insurance company and AIG have taken home millions or billions in compensation packages. So the American public is happy because they were not trapped by a single payer, socialized Medicare, and the CEOs are happy with their severance pay and bonuses.

Similar scenarios could happen if we unsocialized (privatized) our fire departments, our school systems, police forces, and courts. Imagine! The taxpayers would pay for the debacles, but we would have more millionaires.

So down with socialized public services, especially Medicare, Kiddy Care, and any future encroachments into private enterprise! Insurance companies and HMOs, in business for profit, not health, are fervently campaigning and lobbying against further socialization. We don't want wasteful government programs that run on 1% overhead. We as patriotic capitalists prefer to pay those deserving insurance companies their 30% off the top of every healthcare dollar so they can buy advertising, political favors, and huge pay packages for their executive "talent". Let's show the insurance companies and HMOs our support against the evils of more public programs like Medicare. Universal care for Americans? Horrors! This has been the death of me, but hey, I died for a cause and helped cut taxes.

Is this a great country or what?

ARLAND R. MEADE

Written: 2-1-2009

U.S. Economy Is in Dire Straits

The U.S. economy is in dire straits and some solutions have been proposed by our highest experts and officials.

These procedures form what I have dubbed the "hurricane theory." My highest title is professor emeritus, University of Connecticut, and my field was in communications, not economics. Therefore you'll no doubt find flaws in my theory. But would you care to whirl around in it with me?

First, Americans "benefit" from an over-abundance of easy credit. We overbuy, often unwisely. With realization came disaster to our financial system. So to alleviate our predicament, the federal government appropriates $700 billion for lending institutions to use to get us back into more credit, which had caused the calamity in the first place. Not much happens except a few banks folded and others merged to make the huge huger.

Next, our next administration will reduce taxes across the board, but for some more than others. This will, they say, "leave more money in our pockets." We can then get a bit more credit, but mostly spend more on cheap imported goods from Asia.

Our treasury will make up for the lost revenue by selling bonds to Asians and a few oil producers.

The next proposed step is to distribute up to at least $1 trillion to states and individuals to stimulate the economy. (We called this "pump priming" under FDR. Forgive me for being 93 years of age and remembering how we primed water pumps.)

Of course, our treasury doesn't have that money so we'll go further into debt to somebody offshore. Comes the day, ouch! when China needs some money and demands that we redeem the bonds, our debt. We don't have the cash, so we are forced to settle by mortgaging Alaska, California and Texas. Perhaps even Florida, over protest from Cuba.

As the hurricane continues, China forecloses and owns those states. One might be a bit nervous. I'm not eager to see what my next 93 years will be from my hurricane economic theory.

ARLAND R. MEADE

Published: the Polk County Democrat 1-21-2009

Faulty Grammar in High Society

When the president of the University of Florida publicly stated "A special program for my wife and I" (Note the "for I" instead of "for me") a (Lakeland) Ledger reader wrote to decry this improper grammar by a university president. (See Voice of the People, December 1, 2008).

Such usage sets a bad example for our children and immigrants, legal or otherwise, but it has company in unexpected places.

Recently President Elect Obama's choice for the cabinet as Secretary of Education stated on television that his parents "gave my sister and I a good education". I wonder. Note the "gave I", instead of "gave me".

Furthermore, I've heard President Obama Elect include the same faulty use of the nominative "I" instead of the objective case "me".

Now I'm sure we do not want the best grammarian in the country to be our president – she or he might be a dud in everything else. But we should expect better from officials high in educational positions. Or perhaps it doesn't matter. If so, we could be economical and save money by not hiring teachers to teach our children and immigrants English grammar. (They do that, don't they?)

We could reduce the appropriations for education and simply tell people to take their cues from our educational big wigs.

Let's be practical.

ARLAND R. MEADE

Written: 12-11-2008

How to Avoid Social Medicine

A recent hospital experience may have saved my life. The ordeal surely cost thousands of dollars and I received no bill. This is because of the one-payer, universal health care FOR SENIORS, named Medicare. Whatever the label, it is socialized medicine, a term that makes many citizens sick.

This is not, according to insurance companies, the proper American way to provide health care. They expound that the proper way is through their many privatized plans. They fill the airways and our mailboxes with solicitations for such insurance. We love that.

Now there are 2 scenarios, proper according to those afraid of socialized medicine.

Scenario 1: When young I digest hours of TV ads and read bushels of brochures and choose a private health insurance plan. I choose a plan backed by an insurance company, let's say, AIG. Then in 2009 when an affliction happens, I get treatment and the insurance plan should pay the bill. But Whoa! The insurance company is bankrupt. Not to worry! The US taxpayers will bail it out, so the taxpayer pays my medical bill anyway.

Scenario 2: Years ago I decided not to take out any form of medical insurance. I'm healthy and I use the premium to buy stocks. Comes 2009. I'm in agony in an emergency room. Always the first question is "What is your insurance?" Me have insurance? Who, me? No way!

Now I don't know how decisions are made in hospitals, but I presume they do not want many bodies there becoming corpses. So, steps are taken to save my life.

Of course surgeons and medical staff must be paid, so the hospital may prorate what it spent on me among several other patients who had the money to pay, or insurance which could pay – thus requiring others to pay for my hospital costs. But happy accounting, they have avoided that dreaded socialized medicine! Someone or some government agency pays when I can't, or won't.

And, we are told, up to 30 percent of the premiums are overhead, while the socialized medicine for seniors (Medicare) needs one to three percent for administrative expenses. So let's side with the million dollar CEOs who insist on privatized commercial plans. Millionaires have need too.

What a wonderful illogical nation we live in!

ARLAND R. MEADE

Written: 12-9-2008

High School, College Not Path to Better Pay In Global Economy

Too many public figures are spouting off that our schools are broken, and that if we manage to get a much higher rate of high school and college graduation, lo, our workers will get more and higher-paying jobs, and solve our imbalance in international trade.

Let's play with numbers. Suppose we get a few million more high school and college graduates. Then we look at our stores and find that most of our goods are made in Asia. And we note that, for example, the textile and footwear industries have almost vanished from the United States. Was this because too many of our students did not finish high school?

How many of the workers in China who make the goods we want graduated from high school? Or even ever attended one? How many of those factory workers hold college degrees?

Will an increase in high school graduates in this country rush to work in factories at wages allowing our factories to compete on an even basis with those in China? In what galaxy are our "education is everything" preachers from?

There are certainly good reasons for more secondary education for many. We might prefer to live in a community in which all the residents hold high school diplomas rather than in a community where few do. But this is cultural and social, and does not solve an economic crisis.

Let us endeavor to help those who want more formal education, but do it for reasons other than pie-in-the-sky economic fantasy. And, by the way, is the school system broken, or is the society around it broken?

ARLAND R. MEADE

Published: the Lakeland Ledger 12-5-2008

No Cure for Human Nature

Many of us recall that the Reagan Republicans were fond of repeating that government is not the solution, it was the problem. We heard similar assertions as late as the recent presidential campaign.

Well, few are now proclaiming that too much government caused the current financial problem; often we hear that the problem was a lack of government oversight and/or regulation.

So now the "too much government" side is eagerly urging the government to solve, or at least mitigate, the problem. Now, it seems, that the government is the solution, not the problem – a 180 degree shift.

Would it be too daring to suggest that the government is neither the problem nor the solution? What people do, human nature, creates problems. And will solve them. Did a cartoonist once assert that we have met the enemy and it is us? There is no cure for human nature.

ARLAND R. MEADE

Published: the Lakeland Ledger 11-26-2008

Leadership

Why can't the Democrats realize that a hockey mom who has been governor for almost two years and is commander of the National Guard in Alaska (because the law says she is required to be) is qualified to be elected to the office one elderly heartbeat away from the presidency?

Republicans can see this clearly – except perhaps a few hockey moms who would rather not be classed as pit bulls with lipstick.

Why can't everyone see this? What's wrong with the Democrats, anyway?

ARLAND R. MEADE

Published: the Lakeland Ledger 10-3-2008

In Defense of 'Snuck'

On June 9, 2008, a reader berated The Ledger ["Bad Grammar 'Snuck' In" letter] for printing the words "Lawmakers Snuck" in a headline ["Lawmakers Snuck in $110M For Pork, Tax Group Says," May 31]. He maintained that The Ledger should be a model for young writers and should never use "snuck." He also claimed that use of the word "snuck" was bad grammar. Nonsense. We may suspect that he does not know the difference between grammar and diction, but let's overlook that and sneak right into snuck. We'll give him credit for being inventive with his "the conjugation sneak, snuck, snack."

It is likely that as a boy in Maine I snuck around some and said as much. Probably today I'd say "sneaked" to conform closer to usage at The University of Connecticut, which, when I retired from there after decades in professional communications, burdened me with the title Professor Emeritus.

But as I'm not a professional grammarian, I searched for "snuck" in my large British-published Chambers Dictionary. The word "snuck" is referenced, of course, and defined. Chambers states that it is North American vernacular. OK. Writing in vernacular is no sin and is often the appropriate way to convey a message.

In our language we have patterns – probably too many (compare with Esperanto).

Children are likely to sense regular forms and from "I don't want to sleep" come up with the logical "Yesterday I sleeped." So we correct them and say they slept not "sleeped." We might even explain that many of our oldest English words don't follow a pattern – and we say "see, saw seen" instead of "see, seed, seed," or "sing, sang, sung," not "sing, singed, singed."

So the smart kid says "I snuck into the bedroom" and we must tell him or her to say "I sneaked into the bedroom." Get the idea?

I agree with the letter writer that newspapers should not stray far from standard uses – unless in needed exact quotes. It makes a difference whether they write "John is bigger than I (am)," rather than "John is bigger than me (am)."

Now probably the lawmakers referred to earlier sneaked something, but the colloquial "snuck" may give it a more realistic connotation. If we stick around the Legislature too long we may get stuck – or will we get sticked? Long live the English language.

ARLAND R. MEADE

Published: the Lakeland Ledger 6-17-2008

Borrow Less from China

I have a suggestion. It follows from the following published facts:

FIRST: Our government is borrowing huge amounts from China to finance our expenditures. Including our war in Iraq.

SECOND: Our administration is spending billions of dollars to repair or rebuild much of what has been destroyed in Iraq since we invaded that nation.

THIRD: Iraq has accumulated about 80 billion dollars from oil revenues, but the U.S. is paying for most of the rebuilding – including millions that are going to Iraqi officials through corruption and theft.

Therefore, I suggest that we borrow less from China, and borrow some of those billions from Iraq. Then we can continue to spend billions in Iraq. This will serve to extend indefinitely the Bush-Cheney-McCain policy to produce a democratic, free enterprise Iraq.

Our present national administration should be able to add that much to its accomplishments so far for Iraq.

ARLAND R. MEADE

Written: 4-4-2008

Free Enterprise

Every Sunday morning I receive the Lakeland Ledger, a fine newspaper. But with it comes an example of horrible damage to our environment. Although my bathroom scale is not precise enough for evidence, it appears that the advertising supplements weigh at least four times that of the news and feature sections.

Now I know that the advertisers have a legal right to use all these pounds of newsprint (our trees are cut for that), and ink of many colors (which require materials that contaminate the earth), and use of extra energy to produce and transport all this material, and trash disposal when we discard these pounds.

This is free enterprise.

But this use of resources is a curse on our country and not necessary. For example, how many column inches and an illustration do I need that this week a head of lettuce is 98 cents instead of 99 cents – or whatever the amount is. If I want lettuce and have enough money (or credit) I'll buy it whether it is 99 cents or at a "big" 10% discount and only 98 cents this week.

I think that 2008 is the year to help our environment, and try common sense, by reducing the extravagant use of ink and newsprint for advertisement that we don't need.

It just might be the year that we will spend all we want to, or have, anyway.

ARLAND R. MEADE

Written: 12-9-2008

Judgment in Our Presidents

What we need in our U.S Presidents is the ability to make decisions based on facts "on the ground". We have an example in our current President.

It has just been reported that President Bush wants to supply Saudi Arabia with some of the latest military equipment. This is, of course, a suitable reward to a nation that brought us Osama Bin Laden (even though he moved to Afghanistan) and which provided most of the hijackers who crashed into our buildings on September 11.

This is the same president who threw us into a long and costly war in Iraq against people who never threatened us and who did not like Bin Laden anyway.

And during a Middle East Tour President Bush was proclaiming that Iran is a threat to the world. Now history has shown that Iran has spent many decades, if not centuries, in NOT attacking anyone and which has an elected president, unlike our buddy Saudi Arabia which won't even let women drive cars.

That's the kind of judgment we want in our presidents.

We can talk tough with Iran while we negotiate with North Korea, because North Korea has atomic weapons and Iran does not. Playing it safe is a quality we like in presidents who protect us.

And the U.S. taxpayers have provided a billion dollars over recent years to Pakistan, which apparently doesn't know or doesn't care that Osama Bin Laden lives there. Maybe the Saudi government with our smart bombs will put an end to Bin Laden. Surely a president must know something we don't. We are in a presidential campaign, and for reasons, no doubt, pay little attention to candidates like Ron Paul and Denis Kucinich who have for years opposed presidential decisions that have been so ruinous to us in money and human suffering.

Of course we know that we get what we vote for, so let's relax and be happy.

ARLAND R. MEADE

Written: 1-20-2008

Freedom to Speak

Freedom to speak reveals that we'll hear from the most informed to the least informed of this nation, and that is as it should be.

But still, we should be dismayed by what some people say, or write. For example, indignant persons proclaim that the US should keep the federal government out of health care but that no one should touch "our Medicare". They show complete ignorance of the fact that their beloved Medicare is completely paid for by the federal government, that is, by our taxes.

Recently a major TV network news program included a comment stating that we should send more troops to Afghanistan to kill those people, because those people are murderers who like to kill us. The person clearly thought that Afghanistan had attacked the United States. (Perhaps with its superior navy or air force.)

What would be needed to convince her that the attackers were Arabians and not Afghani? And that they took flight training in the United States, used no guns to capture four US aircraft and fly them into targets. Could these mountain tribesmen care? Surely this was not an Afghan project. Many of them do know that Americans are the major customers for drugs made from Afghan-grown poppies.

Anyway, the Arabian perpetrators are gone from Afghanistan, or never were there. I've never seen any statement that any Afghan citizen has killed any American who was not in their country in connection with our invasion of their country. I'm sure they feel justified in killing invaders. They likely call Americans murderers when our bombs and drones kill their children and others.

I wonder who would be guilty if Jesus would be the judge of actions in Afghanistan.

ARLAND R. MEADE

Written: 11-27-2007

Cost of War

While in Australia a few days ago, President Bush proclaimed that the United States was "kicking some butts" in Iraq. This is pretty lowbrow talk coming from a head of state, but then, this was George W. Bush talking.

For the moment, let's assume that GWB is correct, and that he is kicking some butts that need kicking. But think of how much every kick is costing Americans.

We have paid with about 4,000 military lives lost, thousands wrecked by terrible injuries and about a half trillion dollars in cash.

That price is much too high for each butt kicked in Iraq.

ARLAND R. MEADE

Published: the Lakeland Ledger 9-20-2007

Who Are the Insurgents?

Definitions, please!

After years of reading the news and hearing it on television and radio, one assumes that the United States military in Iraq is fighting against "insurgents".

But who are the insurgents? I don't hear or see any definitions given.

Sometimes Sunnis attack Shias, and vice versa. Which of these are the insurgents?

Sometimes we may shoot members of Al Qaeda. Are these insurgents? Who are the insurgents "insurging" against? The United States troops? If that is the case, if we were not there, there might be no insurgents?

General Petraeus reported that Al Qaeda is encouraging some Sunni tribes to fight against the Shias. If Al Qaeda is bent on attacking non-Muslims, then why is Al Qaeda encouraging fellow Muslims to fight against each other? Which of these groups are the "insurgents"?

Civil wars are the nastiest wars: Witness the Spanish Civil War and our own Civil War, more properly called "the War Between the States". In our War Between the States, a soldier's enemy might be his brother, but at least he knew what uniform he wore.

I wish our government officials and the media would be specific in identifying the insurgents.

ARLAND R. MEADE

Written: 4-15-2007

Texas, Presidents and War

Our problems in Iraq are sometimes blamed on Republicans, sometimes on Democrats. This can appear to be a difference in political party leadership. But let's look at a bit of history.

The previous misconceived war in Vietnam was fought to keep that nation divided into two nations. It failed, and we lost about 58,000 lives and who knows how many of our troops are still suffering from terrible injuries.

Then note that fiasco was overseen by a Democratic president – Lyndon Baines Johnson, using false statements about the alleged attack on an American vessel in the Gulf of Tonkin, referred to as the Gulf of Tonkin incident.

Move to today. We have in Iraq a less bloody fiasco, but one more costly in money and world standing. Note that this was promoted by a Republican president, George W. Bush, who, with bias, selected false elements from intelligence reports to justify an invasion of a Muslim nation. We know that we are now in the middle of a religious war – maybe with some oily aspects.

So, stupid invasions of foreign nations are not particularly either by a Democratic or Republican president. But take note that these two big ones were both overseen by a president from Texas.

Therefore, we should turn our attention to the source of our presidents. Perhaps we could prevent such fiascos by passing a constitutional amendment specifying that this country not allow any Texan to be elected our president.

Nothing ventured, nothing gained.

ARLAND R. MEADE

Published: the Lakeland Ledger 2-24-2007

Mysterious People from Outer Space?

I may just be a stickler for terms, but I do wish that the media would be more precise about uses of the words Sunni, Shia, Kurds, or "insurgents" for example.

Typically writers and speakers in the media refer to Sunni, Shia, and Kurd as three entities in the Iraq struggle. The Kurds are Muslim – or at least were half a century ago when I worked in Iraq for more than a year. Therefore they must be either Sunni or Shia. Whichever they are, does that affect how they deal with others in Iraq, or with the Americans, or how we should deal with them?

A bigger fault in the American media is the use of the word "insurgent".

As used, one must presume that the insurgents come from outer space. We frequently read that the Iraqis and Americans killed a certain number of insurgents.

One of our generals stated that perhaps as many as 5% of the insurgents came from outside Iraq, this establishing that 95% of them are Iraqis. And they may be "insurging" against us, but that is not wholly clear. If Sunnis are killing Shias, and Shias are killing Sunnis in a sort of civil war, and we are killing "insurgents", are we killing Sunnis or Shias, or both – or simply these mysterious people from outer space who are neither Shias nor Sunnis, or even Kurds. Does it matter which of these two branches of Islam we are killing?

We are, of course, for the good guys and against the bad guys. Have we declared which of those sects is good? Or maybe neither unless they are Kurdish.

Inasmuch as we have spent more than 400 billion dollars on this war, I wish that the media – or maybe the White House – would make this clear to me, even though it will be our children – not elderly me – who are stuck with the debt.

ARLAND R. MEADE

Written: 1-11-2007

'Brief Period of Discomfort' Is Okay

This note is about your editorials, especially the one published on Dec, 28, 2006, "Focus on the Victim, Not the Perpetrator."

I agree all the way.

An "eye for an eye" approach wasn't suggested and probably should not be followed, but I agree with the writer that a brief period of discomfort by the perpetrator while dying for a heinous crime pales in comparison to that of the victim.

I have been reading and approving almost all of the Democrat's editorials in the Democrat for the seven years I've resided in Bartow after retiring as a professor emeritus from the University of Connecticut.

The editorials have shown what I'll call practical wisdom as well as compassion, and broad and deep knowledge. That the publisher and I typically vote for different political parties is not relevant in this appraisal.

Wisdom is wisdom.

I don't know what the shifting of ownership of the Democrat will do to its editorials, but I do want to record my appreciation that they have been written during my years in Bartow.

ARLAND R. MEADE

Published: the Polk County Democrat 1-2-2007

Detainees Need Trials

On being informed that three prisoners at Guantanamo Bay had committed suicide, President Bush immediately expressed concern that the bodies "were treated humanely and with cultural sensitivity."

What a sweet man!

We are now likely, I suppose, to hear that President Bush will request that the prisoners humanely be allowed one message a year from their families — after we let the families know where their loved ones are.

Then, heaven be praised, we may hear that the prisoners will be permitted to have a court trial — either in the United States or Afghanistan.

Perhaps a couple of them mysteriously invaded the United States on that terrible Sept. 11. No doubt some of them defended that Taliban government that we so reasonably despised. But it was their government, their religion.

Is our president and government afraid of bringing them to trial in what used to be the American way?

ARLAND R. MEADE

Published: the Lakeland Ledger 6-19-2006

Save U.S. Oil Via Importation

How about a radical solution to the petroleum problem of the United States of America?

Let's approach it from an entirely, repeat entirely, selfish viewpoint.

We could establish a policy that most protects our own grandchildren, and lets those in the remainder of the world be damned. How selfish can you get?

The supply of petroleum from the earth is finite. We will exhaust it in a few decades, and the world will suffer unbelievable catastrophe. The pie-in-the-sky word "ethanol" will never save us — the burgeoning population will need to eat that corn, either directly or through livestock.

So the United States should now cap our oil wells, cease our own petroleum extraction and import as much as possible, buying on the world market. We can afford more than most countries can. And we must selfishly conserve our own petroleum resource — for our own self-interest.

Then when world oil supplies are nearly depleted, as they will be, we'll still have some under the ground or sea. Our grandchildren will suffer less than those in the rest of the world.

I said the plan was 100 percent selfish for the United States.

Of course, millions of oil-deprived people will find enough to flood the United States with so many millions of illegal immigrants that our current "undocumented" problem will be a Sunday school picnic.

Well, one can't have everything.

ARLAND R. MEADE

Published: the Lakeland Ledger 5-26-2006

Run Government Like Which Business?

Speculating about operations that deal in millions or billions of dollars is more intriguing to me than, for example, the difference between price of Florida and California strawberries in local stores.

So when the Wall Street Journal reported last week that the recently retired chief executive officer of the company now known as Exxon-Mobil was "compensated" more than $687 million over the past 12 years – a rate of $144,573 per day while he was CEO – I reflected on the declaration I often hear that "Government should be run like a business."

Many highly placed government officials probably would agree. They, like corporate chief executive officers, oversee billion-dollar operations. If they were paid on a basis similar to the Exxon chief, our President Bush, for example, would likely receive at least a half billion dollars a year rather than the measly about $400,000 that is provided to him.

We can find plenty of examples. The current CEO of Home Depot was compensated $14.5 million for a recent year. Should we presume that he is more valuable to our nation than our President is? Should we run our nation like a business and reward the nation's chief executive officer with $14 million every year? How much should the head of our Internal Revenue Service receive? His "enterprise" is bigger than is Home Depot or Exxon.

It happens that I own a bit of Exxon-Mobile stock that currently pays about 1.9 percent dividends. If Exxon's president received compensation as our President does, my dividend might go up a decimal or two.

But my little speculation is not about a possible extra dollar for me, but on the amazing statement by many that "Government should be run like a business."

I presume that they do not mean what they say, but intend to mean that government should be run as efficiently as a business. Maybe so, but when a car manufacturer spends multimillions a year on promotion in hope that I will buy a new car sooner, or hands out $144,573 a day to one person, I question even that position.

ARLAND R. MEADE

Published: the Polk County Democrat 4-24-2006

Presidential Confidence

On the recent day that our newspaper stated that President Bush would seek $91 billion more to conduct the wars in Afghanistan and Iraq "at least through September," I received a solicitation from the Wounded Warriors Project.

This is one of several organizations purporting to provide benefits to our military veterans beyond what we do through our government agencies. It solicits donations for what it wants to do.

Families of the dead and wounded justly want to feel that their loved ones died or became mutilated fighting for their country against nations that threatened us with weapons of mass destruction, etc. — even if the weapons were box cutters and our own planes.

Pundits tell us that President Bush will now devote more attention to domestic affairs, so-called. Think of what he may accomplish given his record in foreign ventures.

His policies and leadership have already stabilized the Middle East, created a democratic government in Iraq and created millions of new friends among Muslims — and, of course, rid Iraq of weapons of mass destruction.

He decided to invade Iraq because he maintained that somehow Saddam Hussein was involved in the Sept. 11 attack he frequently mentions. Of course, he is smart enough not to believe those liberal findings that the attackers were mostly from Saudi Arabia and not one from Iraq, and that the oil profits would not quickly pay our cost for invading Iraq.

Surely this is the leadership mentality that we should rely on to propose policies for our domestic as well as our foreign ventures. Nothing can go wrong . . . go wrong . . . go wrong . . .

ARLAND R. MEADE

Published: the Lakeland Ledger 3-8-2006

71

Practical or Principle?

The debate between people who believe in acting on principle and those who believe on acting to be practical has probably been going on since humans could talk.

The problem of oil in the world is a topic for such debate now.

The Oct. 2, 2005 issue of the Ledger's Parade stated that currently Iraq can't refine enough oil to meet its needs and the American military has to bring in oil to run its vehicles, and that significant oil production is probably five years off. Was this situation brought about by action based on principle or practicality?

President Bush steadfastly insists that we must "stay the course" we started until Iraq becomes a democracy. That sounds more a matter of principle than of practicality.

Before we invaded Iraq, that nation was controlled by a dictatorial government that we found very repulsive. A practical solution back when we were fooling around with that weapons of mass destruction illusion would have been to let the United Nations continue its inspections, and let the Iraqi people revolt, if they wished to enough, against the dictator. Citizens of various nations have done that, even the American 13 Colonies of Britain. Also, in spite of various sanctions, Iraq was exporting considerable oil.

But the Bush-Cheney-Halliburton supporters are determined that Americans will fight there until democracy is established in Iraq. We certainly don't want to buy oil from a country that is not a democracy, do we?

So President Bush acted on principle, not oil. We regret that his decisions are now costing billions, filling our veteran's hospitals with wounded, and killing who knows how many innocent Iraqi citizens. But principle is principle, right?

And who has more principle that the Bush-Cheney-Halliburton trio?

ARLAND R. MEADE

Published: Polk County Democrat 10-18-2005

Presidential Fuel Usage

Recently, a fairly long article in The Ledger stated concern that President Bush and his entourage were using too much fuel in his record as the most-traveled president in history. This is not only for Air Force One, but the caravans on the ground, the required police escorts, other security, and so on.

Although I think the president's nonstop campaigning to hand-picked Republican or military audiences is unnecessary at best, the amount of fuel used is small compared to that our military forces and civilian support are using in Iraq in President Bush's war.

I wonder how we might use here the gasoline we use in Iraq. I think about how much we burned and wasted in the long war in even-more-distant Vietnam. That one provided no U.S. benefit, and it is likely neither will our war in Iraq.

ARLAND R. MEADE

Published: the Lakeland Ledger, 9-18-2005

Flag Burners Arouse Patriotism

This letter is to say that I greatly appreciate your editorial in the June 27, 2005 issue headed "Our Flag Does Not Need Constitutional Protection."

You express a deep understanding of history and of Americans. I realize that "desecration" does not automatically mean flag burning, although that is the conclusion many citizens erroneously jump to.

Whatever gain those who do "desecrate" may obtain is more than offset by the anger against them by others; this actually increasing respect for our flag. And the occurrences are too rare to concern the Constitution anyway.

ARLAND R. MEADE

Published: The Polk County Democrat 7-8-2005

Social Security Shock and Awe

Recently President Bush conducted a sort of "shock and awe" campaign across our nation to advance his wish to privatize some of our social security program.

He did this with the same enthusiasm and confidence he demonstrated when he was seeking world and USA support for the invasion of Iraq. I'm convinced that he is a born leader.

So, why should he be scoring less than 50 percent in the opinion polls?

He has proved his good judgment and vision by eliminating weapons of mass destruction in Iraq (overlooking the box cutters and the Arabian attackers of our Twin Towers and the Pentagon).

His diplomatic skills have reduced the number of those in the world who oppose our policies, proving he is a consensus builder. (Let's not list the nations that don't agree.) He has fulfilled his promise to speedily capture Osama Bin Laden. (Well, there is still time.)

He has stabilized Iraq and the Middle East (Well, the Saudi Arabian part, almost – let's not be picky).

He has promoted policies that have increased our favorable balance of trade. (Don't believe statistics that report the opposite).

He has presided over policies that have reduced our national debt. (That's why Congress has to increase the legal debt limit now and then).

He has made steps toward less spending in our national budget. (It wouldn't be sporting, would it, to note that the billions spent on the Iraq and Afghanistan wars are not included in the budget?)

He has former dictator Hussein in prison. (No doubts here. No, the President is not responsible for the pictures of Saddam wearing only briefs).

With all these examples of President Bush's intelligent and informed leadership, Americans must admire him and agree with his campaign to put some of our retirement money into such safe places as Wall Street investments. What could go wrong, go wrong, and go wrong?

ARLAND R. MEADE

Published: the Lakeland Ledger 5-24-2005

What Does God Need?

In the letters section of the December 7 Ledger, a writer brings forth a concept that is novel, to me at least. He stated that "We need and GOD NEEDS our elected president to carry on and promote peace in place of terror."

God NEEDS? NEEDS? What happens when God is needy? Does the Almighty, the one who created the universe, really need George W.? If Ohio had voted for nominee Kerry, would God then need President Kerry?

The world has experienced centuries with cruel dictators who slaughtered millions and starved millions of children to death. There has always been more than enough terror. Who did God need during those years? Perhaps the Jews in Germany needed God during the holocaust period.

Some contributors to the Ledger believe that we have put God out of the public schools. They confuse their God with Mr. Milquetoast. God will be in any schoolroom or anywhere else He wishes. Who can defy the Almighty?

Of course governments can and sometimes do take sponsored or directed sectarian prayers out of public schools, or put them in. Religious people are most effective in putting them into schools. They sometimes use force to make everyone kowtow to their religious believes, include the Taliban of Afghanistan, The Wahabi of Saudi Arabia, and the Christians of Maryland in 1649 when they passed the so called Maryland's Tolerance Act. That one is worth thinking through.

The "Tolerance Act" was more than three centuries ago, but that is about 16 centuries since the beginning of Christianity. It included: "…Whatsoever person or persons within this province …shall from henceforth blaspheme God… or shall deny our Savior Jesus to be the Sonne of God, or shall deny the Holy Trinity, the Father, Sonne and Holy Ghost, or the Godhead of any of the said Three persons of the Trinity or the trinity of the Godhead… shall be punished with death and confiscation or forfeiture of all his or her lands." Don't skip over that punishment by death provision. Or that someone wanted to get land without buying it.

Such people believe that God "needs" them to perpetuate such nonsense and cruelties in His name – whatever the name that such people give to their chosen God. Or does the Devil make them do it?

Scary isn't it? God help us!

ARLAND R. MEADE

Published: the Lakeland Ledger 12-12-2004

Veterans Undergarments

In the November 11, 2004 Ledger I read the article under the headline "Underclothes Needed for Vets."

The stated need was for veterans at a veteran's hospital in Tampa.

According to a leader in the month-long drive for these items, "There really isn't anyone to take care of these guys." Really?

During recent years our "compassionate conservative" government has readily spent billions for bombers and tanks to spread bombs and bullets on and into residents of a country that never threatened us – the one whose vicious dictator was no fan of the theocratic Osama Bin Laden and his gang.

Are we to assume that these compassionate conservatives could not afford to deliver underwear to needy veterans-veterans who include men and women wounded, even maimed for life, in such a war?

Of course we will as individuals step forward to help. We might even, later, find ways to provide underwear for the thousands of Iraqis who have become or will become sick and disabled veterans.

I wonder whether the article mentioned will be picked up by the European press, maybe with such leads as "United States citizens asked to donate underwear to veterans, because the hundreds of billions spent in Iraq didn't leave enough for their underwear."

We know that President Bush indicated that the French are slackers. What do you suppose the French think about our underwear drive and its implications?

ARLAND R. MEADE

Published: the Lakeland Ledger 11-18-2004

Bible Reading Can't Be Banned

On page 26 of November 1, 2004 Newsweek was printed some reports of how low the current Presidential campaign has become in matters of church and religion.

Reports include, "In West Virginia and Arkansas evangelical volunteers received GOP-sponsored pamphlets warning that Bible-reading could be banned if John Kerry won."

The danger is not so much that the sponsors presume that their church member voters are so ignorant – although that is bad enough – but that their voters are so ignorant. No candidate and no party has or would be so foolish as even to suggest a ban on Bible reading for many reasons, including the Constitution of the United States.

That a political party would stoop to such a tactic need not surprise us, although this demonstrates a sorry state of affairs. The perpetrators know that "could be banned" is assuredly a lie. One has to swallow common sense to vote for people, or party, who perpetuate such a statement.

ARLAND R. MEADE

Published: the Polk County Democrat 11-2-2004

Bombed into Submission

I wonder how anyone can question President Bush's belief that a people can be bombed into submission. Look at the precedents for such a belief.

Israel has been bombing houses in Palestine for years, and obviously the Palestinians have folded.

Russia has flattened much in the cities of Chechnya, and the events tell us that they have given up their struggle for independence.

U.S. planes and tanks have dropped more tons of bombs on Iraq than Saddam Hussein ever had, and we note that resistance has collapsed.

Really?

One could imagine that some nations or peoples hate to be occupied by foreign troops.

Is that such a novel idea? I haven't heard the governments of Israel, Russia, or the United States suggest that yet. (Our own history tells us that even the Confederate States of America were not keen on the idea when the occupiers wore blue.)

Our steadfast President says we will continue as long as "necessary", even several years. Why not? We can afford more explosives than the people of the Middle East can. We have already spent 200 billion dollars and a thousand plus lives and thousands of wounded and maimed. But we have more money and more troops than the entire Middle East. Our President proclaims how steadfast he is. And that makes him right?
If you believe that, support the President, and bomb on and on!

ARLAND R. MEADE

Written: 9-14-2004

Murphy's Law

Somewhere near wherever Murphy's Law is, there lurks the Law of Unexpected Consequences.

An article in the July 26 issue of TIME reminds us of a tragic example. The title is "Marked Women." The article reports that after our victory over Iraq, the number of so-called "honor killings" has increased dramatically. This is their term for murders of women by the men of their own families. The women are killed - often by brothers - because the women have or are suspected of having sexual intercourse outside marriage. Although "honor killings" are against national laws, because of cultural beliefs, typically the murderers go unpunished, or receive only by a token slap on the wrist.

That sexual situation hardly raises eyebrows nowadays in most "Western" nations, but is a capital crime in old Middle Eastern cultures. The killing supposedly absolves the family from the shame of the woman's action. That surely a man must have been involved seems overlooked. The killer typically goes free or maybe receives a slap on the wrist.

The practice is not limited to Iraq. But the irony is that the secular dictatorship of Saddam Hussein had reduced the frequency of such killings. Killers were tried and usually imprisoned up to three years. Since his ouster, there has been some reverting to the ancient custom. That three-year imprisonment seems a trivial penalty to us in America, but without the secular dictatorship, the killers are usually punished not at all. The murders are considered a family matter.

TIME reports that Iraqi parents fear that racy TV shows and the internet - outlawed under Saddam - are influencing boys toward sexual behavior. Maybe so, but the young women are the ones punished horribly for "straying." Or appearing to.

Surely prostitution has long existed in the Middle East and around the world. In 1952-53 when I resided in Baghdad as a public information official for President Truman's Point Four Program (AID), my family lived within sight and sound of an establishment that seemed like a casino, but which was more, we assumed, than that. Whatever one thinks of prostitutes, one must, it seems to me, feel ashamed of a human culture where not only prostitutes, but women who are not, are freely murdered for participating equally, almost, with men, who often are not punished at all.

We can hope that even if the next government of Iraq is controlled by the religious fundamentalists, as is possible, some moves against this killing of women can be reinstated and strengthened.

ARLAND R. MEADE

Published: the Polk County Democrat 8-2-2004

Special Gas Tax Would Defray Costs of War

Gasoline prices have reached $5.79 per gallon in England, according to The Ledger of June 3, 2004. The pumps in England are not calibrated in gallons, but I presume someone carefully calculated the rate to $5.79 American.

Gasoline prices in the United States are a few cents over $2 and edging up slowly.

Our country has spent about $200 billion on the Iraq war, and the president has asked for $25 billion more. I don't know how much the United Kingdom has poured into this venture.

Now the present administration seems indifferent to how high our national debt reaches, and presumably having our children pay for our war is OK with this administration and many others.

Perhaps paying as we spend is not feasible. But the concept is at least noble. A few Americans suffer the maximum for this war; most of us suffer very little, if any.

So I suggest that we take one step toward being reasonable to our children, and do the following: legislate a national 10 cents a gallon federal tax with the entire proceeds used to defray the costs of this war. Many will scream at any more tax on gasoline, but isn't fairness still a part of American beliefs?

Europeans will note that hurting only to the extent of 10 cents per gallon makes us pikers — but President Bush a year ago indicated that the European countries were in that category, so what do we care!

I propose that this special tax be terminated on the date that the United States has no more troops stationed in Iraq, Germany and Japan.

ARLAND R. MEADE

Published: the Lakeland Ledger 6-12-2004

We Were Once Revolutionaries

Wars are fought with words as well as guns. Guns are straightforward and we all know that they will kill. Words can be false, malicious, or simply stupid. And kill. Our 500 pound bombs do more damage than muskets, but the principles are the same.

Recently President Bush has told us that Iraqis are shooting at our troops because they are occupying their nation; and at our planes because for a decade we have been flying over it. Maybe they want freedom from foreign troops more than they want freedom to vote.

There are precedents. One is when citizens of Massachusetts, then part of the British Empire, shot at British soldiers from behind trees and stone walls – a form of ambush. We now call those citizens patriots. The British had other names for them.

Iraqis are shooting at occupying troops and no doubt use ambush and other maneuvers that we hate.

George, the President, calls them thugs and worse.

George, the British King, called the Americans traitors and would have hanged any of them or their leaders if caught.

George, the President, has ordered leaders of the Iraqi resistance killed if they can't be readily captured, even heads of state – a precedent.

Our patriots were thugs to the British government; their patriots are the thugs to our government. The difference is in the scale, not in kind.

It is safe to say that not all Iraqis did agree with their government; and did not agree with ours either. Neither did all the people in the Colonies favor our armed citizens, or militia, shooting from behind walls at marching British troops.

Whether we call the Iraqis simply insurgents against an occupying force, or thugs or haters of freedom, words will be used by both sides for propaganda and moral functions – and history.

President Bush assures us that God is on our side. The Iraqis know beyond a doubt that Allah is on their side. Wish that we could settle the conflict with a duel of those Powers, as did knights of old. Or would that simply be an internal conflict within the One God? Only God / Allah knows.

ARLAND R. MEADE

Published: the Polk County Democrat 4-22-2004

Is Location in Religion Important?

Often we hear that business success is in location, location, location. A sort of trinity – with a lower case "t". I don't recall hearing a theologian or church leader proclaiming that as critical in a religion. Why not?

In periods of Easter, Christmas, and sometimes weekly, we are reminded that some 2000 years ago God chose an unmarried Semitic girl named Mary to be the mother of His Only Begotten Son. Millions have no problem with that. But consider how absolutely critical the location was.

The Jewish maiden lived in an area of the Roman Empire, and among a people who had a written language – although there is no record that Mary could read or write. No matter. The story not only spread by word of mouth but more importantly, decades later, by the written word that could be translated and passed on through the centuries, as in various chapters of our Bible.

Now suppose that God had chosen a maiden of the Iroquois people in New York – or whoever their ancestors were in that area – to mother his Only Begotten Son. The same or similar story could have been in the folklore of the Iroquois, but never written by them – they had no written language and none of them traveled to Rome.

Centuries later when Europeans, of whatever faith (It could not have been Christian) discovered the New World and heard the tale, they would not have believed it any more than they believed other tales the Indians told about how the Great Spirit created mankind.

So the world would never have had the New Testament and its story of the Son of God. Now that is critical in many ways.

We can't know how many pogroms, pilgrimages, crusades, holy wars, burnings at the stake, etc. might have been eliminated. We cannot know what religion would predominate in the United States. What church would President Bush attend? He could never have heard of Jesus. Would it matter? Would we have the same opinions on the separation of church and state? And if separate church and state would be an issue, what kind of church?

In religion as in business, don't ignore… location, location, location.

ARLAND R. MEADE

Written: 4-7-2004

Black Smudge on American Honor

Ledger readers, did you fail to read the editorial in the Nov. 8, 2003 edition? If you did, I urge you to go to wherever you stashed or discarded that issue, find it, and read the editorial. The title is "The Nonpersons of Guantanamo."

The editorial concludes with the suggestion that unless we treat the captives we hold at guantanamo as people, our actions make the United States "simply a hostage taker."

Read the entire editorial please. Our administration's current actions are placing a black smudge on American Honor.

Our captives, of course, supported a government and party whose positions and activities we hated. It was, however, their government, not ours. With our superior military power, we are able to capture some who logically fought back when we invaded their nation.

As hateful as we deem the Taliban, when we capture their soldiers, they are enemy combatants, and we should treat them according to the Geneva Conventions. We did that much when we captured German and Japanese soldiers while we were fighting Hitler and the Japanese Emperor.

Our administration believes that it is above international law. We will not benefit by continuing this position.

ARLAND R. MEADE

Published: the Lakeland Ledger 11-15-2003

Spending for Iraq

I read that President Bush's request for U.S. spending in Iraq includes an item of $400 million to build two prisons at a rate of $50,000 per bed. Perhaps we should say "bedroom" or "cell."

We have built what some call "cages" at Guantanamo, Cuba, to house captured Afghanis. I don't know the cost per cage, but I expect that it is less than $50,000 per prisoner, although the cost doesn't include any mail service or other means to contact families back home.

Of course, I have no clue on the number of Iraqis that our administration intends to lock up in Iraqi prisons. (I assume that the old ones are decrepit), but $50,000 per bed seems a bit luxurious.

When I lived in Iraq very, very long ago — as a technical aid information officer — I noted that bricks can be easily and abundantly made there. And that bricks are the principal building material. Surely there are many unemployed men who would gladly do the building at much less than U.S. wages. I presume that we must include substantial overhead and profits for some American contractor.

Reducing Iraqi unemployment would be compassionate, but is the President's proposal really a good way to spend American tax dollars?

ARLAND R. MEADE

Published: the Lakeland Ledger 10-10-2003

Ask Saddam for Help

It has been recently announced that the United States will destroy tons of its sarin nerve gas and other poisons.

The President of the United States has told us that such gasses are weapons of mass destruction – at least when they are held by other nations.

I believe that the U.S. Army and its scientists know how to safely destroy such gasses; by incinerating, it has been announced.

Many people in Alabama, where the destruction is scheduled to start, have their doubt.

They are worried.

But there may be another way. Somewhere in the Middle East, address uncertain, is someone who has proved to be adept at making weapons of mass destruction disappear right before our eyes. His name is, the last we knew, Saddam Hussein.

Perhaps before we worry the citizens of Alabama so much, we should question him.

ARLAND R. MEADE

Published: the Polk County Democrat 9-4-2003

Rebuilding Iraq

We teach children to be responsible for their decisions — or should — and that they should take the consequences for misbehavior.

We should expect our nation to be responsible for its actions and to take the consequences for its misbehavior.

Now that we are faced with huge financial and other problems in what we call rebuilding Iraq (I wonder who unbuilt it?) our leaders are suggesting that other nations of the world should help us. Why?

The conquest of Iraq was pushed by our government leaders over the objections of most of the world nations. And we ridiculed such nations as Germany, Mexico, and France and most of the United Nations when they would not join us. Now we'd be glad if they helped us undo the damage. What a copout!

This war and its results are the responsibility of the United States. So what if it will cost us $100 billion or so, and we don't know how many lives. So what if a result of our decision makes our national debt skyrocket, reduces what we might do for education, causes cutbacks in many health programs. So what if many can't get enough prescription medicine — even for elderly Republican women who voted for George W. We are all in this together and should shoulder the consequences.

It is the honorable position to take.

ARLAND R. MEADE

Published: the Lakeland Ledger, 7-30-2003

Show Them a Thing or Two

Recently the world's greatest military power under the brilliant leadership of President Bush quickly smashed the military and government of a feeble nation.

He did this, as he stated, to eliminate a threat to us from weapons of mass destruction and to reduce threats from terrorists. And although he was not able to convince many nations of his position, he initiated the war anyway.

As results of recent days and weeks indicate, he succeeded in reducing attacks by terrorists to almost nil. And of course did this without creating thousands of new enemies.

And neither our troops nor the United Nations team have been able to find any weapons of mass destruction.

I have a suggestion. That one of our so-called allies in this war – let's say Romania or Bulgaria – help by sending a Piper Cub to Iraq to collect the weapons of mass destruction. Secretary of State Powell has repeatedly asserted that he knows where they are. He could guide loading the plane.

Then Bulgaria could fly the plane to France and land on the great mall beside the Palace of Versailles. They could show the French a thing or two by unfurling a huge banner stating in Bulgarian and/or in English Hey You Un-American Frenchmen! We Won! Shame on You for Not Seeing Everything Our Way. And then they would pour a bottle of French wine onto the grass.

I don't know enough about wine to know which variety, but something very expensive would be in order.

ARLAND R. MEADE

Published: the Polk County Democrat 5-27-2003

A Muslim's Prayers

We know that there are at least a few thousand residents of Iraq who are Christians, but that the majority are Muslims.

Muslims typically bow toward Mecca and pray to God five times daily. Of course, we don't know what they are saying in their prayers, but I assume that their words include asking God (by the Arabic word for God) for some sort of help or deliverance.

In this time of destruction and peril, I assume that they are also thanking God. As they witness areas of Baghdad smashed and burned by thousands of American bombs landing at night – some reputed to be as large as 4,500 pounds – they do, I presume, thank God daily that America does not use weapons of mass destruction.

ARLAND R. MEADE

Published: Polk County Democrat 4-3-2003

Obstinate France Aids Iraq by Blocking U.S., U.N., and NATO

Our administration officials, and some others, have told us hundreds of times that one of the reasons for waging war on Iraq is that a decade ago Saddam Hussein gassed to death the inhabitants of several Kurdish village — Iraqi citizens. Some say that as many as 5,000 died.

Our indignation was moderate. Possibly, at that time, the United States should have kidnapped Saddam — as it did President Noriega in Panama a couple of administrations ago. If we then hanged Saddam by the thumbs until dead, that would be OK with me.

Now, after these many years, our compassionate president uses the gassing episode as an excuse to destroy huge amounts of Iraq structure, infrastructure, and with it, unavoidably, kill or maim thousands of Iraqis — none of whom probably gassed any Kurds.

In our president's logic, this is sort of getting even.

The quota is not sure. Perhaps if we kill twice as many non-Kurdish Iraqis as Saddam killed Kurds that would teach him a lesson. In the process, we might capture or kidnap Saddam himself. We could then have him share the cell in the United States with Noriega.

You may remember that we imprisoned Noriega to stop the flow of drugs from Latin America to the United States. That obviously has worked notably well. Perhaps imprisoning Saddam will eliminate hate of the United States and thus cause terrorism to cease.

And, because we are a compassionate nation, we will surely spend billions to rebuild the physical and economic damage we do to Iraq.

Perhaps even our compassionate president could then sleep nights without restoring the thousands we kill.

ARLAND R. MEADE

Published: the Lakeland Ledger 2-15-2003

Economist Tallies Swelling Cost of Israel to U.S.

Under the Christian Science Monitor heading "Economist Tallies Swelling Cost of Israel to U.S.", I find the figure $5,700 per person. That is per person living in the United States today, not the population of Israel. This calculation is based on the one point six TRILLION dollars that Israel has cost the United States since 1973, according to a consulting economist in Washington, D.C. backed by a number of military and diplomatic officials, mostly retired.

For some Americans, spending this much on Israel is OK. It is only money, which we have in abundance. And it does include 50 to 60 billion dollars of private money, although the remainder is direct or indirect from the U.S. taxpayers. Some of the indirect will be when the U.S. Treasury inevitably must cover some 600 billion dollars in commercial and housing loans to Israel. But is it only money? Much of it was for military hardware used to keep Israel's conquered area, where the population is mostly Palestinian, some being Christian, from freedom. Two and a half billion dollars to support Israel's Lavi Fighter and Arrow missile projects is but a sample. And yearly we grant $1.8 billion in military aid, plus providing huge amounts of military equipment at huge discounts.

We can afford all this of course, but can we afford to maintain this destabilizing thorn in the Middle East, creating enemies and terrorists against both us and against Israel? Its damage extends far beyond Palestine.

Israel is there. It will stay. The world must not let Israel or any nation be extinguished by force. But the United States and the rest of the world must force Israel to accept reasonable borders and cease its aim to hold Palestinians in subjugation until Israel's aim to replace them is accomplished.

The Israeli "settlement" aim is pretty clear, but should we be able to sleep at night while spending such huge sums to make that possible?

ARLAND R. MEADE

Written: 12-13-2002

Weapons of Mass Destruction

It is time that decent Americans should be shouting at President Bush that this country does not attack weak nations that have never attached us and, in fact, probably don't have the mass destruction facilities to attack us. Iraq stupidly has attacked Iran (our beloved, if I may be sarcastic) and Kuwait (which isn't particularly friendly to the United States now). But stupidity is hardly justification for being bombed to pieces by the world's most powerful nation.

Terrorists who were almost all from our bosom buddy nation Saudi Arabia committed a horrible crime scene against our people. Therefor – to be sarcastic again – President Bush surely should bomb a country from which NONE of the terrorists originated.

President Bush worries that Iraq may soon have weapons of mass destruction.

Let's publish a list of all nations who have weapons of mass destruction – of course the United States is number one – and decide in which order we will bomb them. Will India be first? Israel? Great Britain? Iraq? Pakistan? This is not a complete list, but one gets the idea of the idiocy of one nation, even ours, deciding to police the world on the basis of weapons of mass destruction.

If we follow the preaching of President Bush, the second one, can we justify the huge cost in lives, oil, dollars, honor, and honesty?

I have not been in Iraq since 1953 (I was there with President Truman's Point Four Program), but I know that it is an exposed, bleak area in which anything big is difficult to hide. There's earth enough to bury a lot, but such spots would likely be readily found. As embarrassing as it is to a nation's pride to have the world search within its borders for hidden weapons, Iraq should again permit the United Nations inspectors to do this.

The problem would likely be solved, and we could go on defending ourselves against, for instance, terrorists like those Saudi citizens – who trained in the United States, and, with box cutters as weapons, hijacked four large airplanes. Instruments of mass destruction?

You know the rest of the story.

ARLAND R. MEADE

Written: 9-13-2002

Esperanto – a Universal Language

Dear Editor:

I appreciate your printing the letter by Prof. Glossop, under the heading "Alternative to 'natural' languages – Esperanto."

Perhaps obvious to today's Americans, but one might mention that one can find much about Esperanto on the internet, in various languages for those who don't already read Esperanto. And although, as Ronald Glossop stated, Esperanto started as a design by Zamenhof, in Poland, it has been greatly amplified in vocabulary and usage, with general and specialized dictionaries in many languages.

I attended one world Esperanto Congress (in Spain) where for a week no other language was used by 1900 persons from 41 nations. Neither translators nor interpreters were available or needed. Does this suggest the great advantage for international events?

A neat little side issue. Our spelling bees, so intriguing in English, would be impossible in Esperanto. The language is 100% phonetic, so after a few hours of orientation, no one could fail to spell any word correctly pronounced, nor fail to pronounce any word correctly spelled.

Thank you.

ARLAND R. MEADE

PS Not relevant to Esperanto, but I'm a professor emeritus from the University of Connecticut, with specialty in agricultural communication.

Mi dankas vin ke vi presis la leteron de Ronald Glossop. Estas trop esperi ke vi presus c'i tiu, sed me esperas. Esperanto estas bona lingvo ke meritas pli atenton kaj uzon. Sincere via, Arland.

Published: Christian Science Monitor 8-11-2002

Establish a Palestininian State

We Americans never had the experience of being conquered and occupied (except for the American Indians). So we have a little difficulty in being in the shoes of a conquered people.

Move to Palestine. Israel conquered all of Palestine "fair and square", in military terms. So the inhabitants should relax and accept it, should they not? Maybe not.

To be basic, let's assume that Premier Sharon is overly rough, and also that Arafat is guilty of most of what Sharon accuses him of. And then assume that by some magic both Premier Sharon and Arafat should vanish from the earth; and that the suicide bombing and some other symptoms (the bombings are symptoms, not causes) also vanish.

Thereupon the basic situation would not change a whit. Millions of Palestinians would still want to be free of Israel and Israeli policy would still be that God gave Palestine to the Jews much more than two millennia ago.

The question for the current world is whether a conquered people should stay conquered or whether they have higher rights – whether the bitterness can go on for a few more hundreds of years, until say, the Old Testament is amended.

I think that President Bush and Secretary of State Powell have it right, when they state that it is time to establish a Palestinian state. I'm not a Bush fan, but he's right on this one.

ARLAND R. MEADE

Published: the Polk County Democrat 5-16-2002

Soldiers Are Worth More

A recent CBS program (Sam Donaldson) reported figures that should make Americans ashamed. It was stated that if one of our military men fighting for our nation in Afghanistan should be killed in action, our government guarantees for his family $8,000 in direct death benefits plus some paltry other sums, which in total are less than one would earn in a year at minimum wage levels.

By contrast, the family of one lost in enemy action on Sept. 11 will probably receive about $1,800,000.

The families of American service men or women killed in the cold mountains of Afghanistan will receive some $12,000 while the families of persons at desk jobs in one of the Twin Towers will become millionaires.

Might the family of the dead soldier feel like second- or third-, or one hundredth-class citizen in comparison? Is the life of a soldier so much less to our nation than the life of a stock broker?

Is this the kind of American fairness to be an example to the world – or to be taught to our children? Has our President and Congress spent a morning thinking about this cruel injustice? Have the rest of us?

ARLAND R. MEADE

Published: the Polk County Democrat 3-14-2002

Don't Waste Money over Iraq

The news this week that the Iraqis shot down one of our unmanned spy planes stimulated the following thoughts.

We know that for about a decade we have spent, unreported, multi-millions in manned flights over so-called "no fly zones" in northern and southern Iraq. Those planes and pilots are still safe, but they cost U.S. taxpayers dearly.

The reported reason is to protect dissident Iraqis – generally Kurds or Muslims of the Shiite branch from dictator Saddam Hussein. When I worked in Iraq as public information officer for the then technical aid program – the one initiated by President Truman and labeled Point Four – I traveled all of Iraq except the northern tip.

How flying planes protect individuals from wrath or injury from Saddam Hussein is beyond me. How we are squandering huge amounts of airplanes fuel and U.S. dollars is clear enough. I know that the money is coming from our billions allocated to national defense. A strange label for defending, perhaps, the house where my family lived in Baghdad: let it go!

This week we also heard that the U.S. Treasury surplus is in question, perhaps disappearing.

I suggest that we cease wasting money over Iraq and spend it, if it is there to spend, on children in this country, or anywhere.

ARLAND R. MEADE

Published: The Polk County Democrat 9-5-2001

Safety Instructions in Esperanto

As did other thousands of Americans this summer, I crossed the Atlantic by plane. And, not remarkably, I read the "safety instructions" card. I also listened to such instructions in three languages. No problem, as English is my native tongue and that was used on the card and by the stewardess who explained. The dominance of English for in-flight instructions is obvious, but uncounted thousands travel by plane who are not familiar with any of those languages.

Knowing this, the airplane companies do what they can by selecting a handful of languages for the printed instructions – I think the number was seven on this flight. For reasons of economy and space, I presume, the print for each was tiny – some passengers would require magnifying glasses of some sort.

As these planes rarely crash, does it matter much? If my mother tongue was one of the hundreds of written languages NOT seeing print on my flight instructions and spoken by NOT ONE of the crew, it might to me. Not feasible were such major languages as Hindi, Malay, Indonesian, Russian, Italian, and so on.

A solution entirely scientific, logical, and feasible would be for a single world language to be ADDED to the five, say, needed by the crew and that would make it easiest for most relevant passenger groups.

Such an easy auxiliary language, as Esperanto, could be taught at a small expense in public schools and to adult groups. In fact, it probably is the only complete language that a person can teach himself or herself in, say, Timbuktu and likewise in the US and be mutually understood the first time they meet – or hear it on an airplane.

As a neutral, easy language it could be acquired readily worldwide with the knowledge that it could have a multitude of international uses, in flight and otherwise. No one would need to kowtow to another's language so there would be no bias. Although 70% of Esperanto's vocabulary can be traced to Latin, it has been constructed to be regular, phonetic, and complete – for both speaking and writing.

This world SECOND language could then be on aircraft safety cards as the one UNIVERSAL language – in addition to the three or four for the major flying population.

Our universe operates on emotion, custom, and power, not on logic. But as the saying goes: "There'll come a day…."

ARLAND R. MEADE

Written: 10-11-2000

Esperanto to the Rescue

At best, communication in tragic conditions is difficult, in any nation, in any language.

At the moment, consider rescue and aid crews from about 20 nations rushing to Turkey in order to rescue or aid thousands hurt and homeless. Receiving, coordinating, and directing them in Turkish would fall on most willing, but most likely not comprehending ears. Also the Turkish first aid workers, police, and all officials could hardly be expected to suddenly be conversant in a dozen or more languages. There have even been reports that the aid crews' first difficulties was with Turkish customs officials.

In the United States, we too, typically, say let all people learn English. We don't need to enumerate the difficulties in that aim – albeit that might be best in many parts of the world. But usually not where the great catastrophes are most likely to happen.

But Red Cross professionals, Red Crescent professionals, and likely rescue and aid groups of various categories could agree on a worldwide mutual language for themselves, namely the regularly constructed and fully developed language ESPERANTO. This would resolve many communication problems. Even a three-day crash course in this absolutely regular, logical, and easy-to-pronounce language would work wonders with those not already prepared when the need came. Also being neutral, no nation would feel second class. Rescue and aid would be expedited.

ARLAND R. MEADE

Written: 8-25-1999

Human Affairs

In human affairs there have been periods when a man had had a too-intimate affair, he was expected to cover it up, even to lie about it, to protect the good name of the lady. That was considered gentlemanly.

Today, if he does the same to cover up the act, that is considered impeachable – especially when the lady talks about it to a snitch with a tape recorder.

ARLAND R. MEADE

Written: 12-10-1998

Esperanto Spoken Here

Readers of the Polk County Democrat have, of course, a variety of experiences in international activities. Can any of them match in kind the following?

I've just sent a ballot to The Netherlands on which I voted for 8 of 16 nominees for a position in an international organization. The candidates I voted for live in Korea, India, Costa Rica, China, Spain, Russia, Israel, and Japan.

I don't know the mother language of any of these candidates, and possibly they don't know mine. But I made my selection after reading many paragraphs with their brief biographies and organizational aims. This was all in the international language Esperanto.

ARLAND R. MEADE

Published: the Polk County Democrat 6-29-1998

Wasting 40 Million Dollars of Taxpayers Money

Has the United States spent 40 million dollars to discover a man who does not need VIAGRA?

The taxpayers paid millions for a Whitewater Investigation that proved Bill and Hilary Clinton lost money in real estate.

We paid millions more and found that Paula Jones may have been invited to see too much of Governor Clinton.

The taxpayers have been billed millions more to find out whether President Clinton revealed too much to a nubile intern. And the end of this bill is not in sight.
Obviously this information is more vital to our government than….. (FILL IN YOUR OWN LONG LIST.)

This is titillating, but what we really bought for our $40,000,000 is the knowledge that a certain successor to the Father of Our Country has not needed one of those blue Viagra pills.

Way to go K. Starr!

You may yet save the nation.

ARLAND R. MEADE

Written: 6-5-1998

U.S. Alone in Boycotting Cuba

I was glad to read that a church-related organization had found a way to circumvent the stupid law that proclaims to the world the United States is the only nation on this globe afraid of Fidel Castro's Cuba (news story, Aug. 30, "Activists defy law, deliver aid to Cuba").

I am not a member of any group involved, nor do I even know whether the Cubans needed the goods shipped. I'm basing my comments on disgust that our government is the only one in the world that denies its citizens rational intercourse with Cubans.

In 1990, the Universal Esperanto Association, headquartered in the Netherlands, held its annual convention in Havana. The association encourages adoption of a neutral auxiliary language called Esperanto for international businesses, diplomacy, travel and so on. Goodwill has always been embedded in Esperantist thinking. Nations welcome its annual conferences. Only 1,617 registered for the conference in Cuba; this year I attended the one in Valencia, Spain, with 1900 other registrants from 61 nations.

But would the U.S. government permit its citizens to go to Cuba for this conference? No. We might, the law supposes, give aid to the "enemy". Some Americans did attend with the help of Mexico, but they had to be sure that they spent not a cent or they would be subject to U.S. criminal penalties. This made us the joke of the world there.

I applaud the bold church people who managed to ship food and medicine to Cuba in spite of our stupid law (with the help of Mexico, again).

Next year, the world Esperanto Congress will be in Seoul, Korea; I presume our government has no objections to our going there. We might even buy Hyundai cars there, instead of buying a car from Detroit. That would be more American , legally, than donating medicine to Cubans.

ARLAND R. MEADE

Published: The Hartford Courant 9-14-1993

Can State Benefit from Casinos?

Can casino gambling make money for Connecticut? Let's count the ways.

There is only one, presuming that the casinos are not able to print money. That one would be to require that all gamblers be from outside Connecticut. That would be neat, as we could have a share of their losses.

Some presume that Connecticut will benefit from the millions that our residents will spend on gambling. That will only move money around. The money will be part of the earnings – or tax-paid benefits – that the Connecticut residents are going to spend for something – say, better schools, shoes, books, vacations, better homes and so on. It is surely not money they draw continually from a pile that would not otherwise be spent.

Now of course if this shifting of money flow in Connecticut produces a share for the Connecticut treasury that would clearly be a tax that the gamblers volunteer to pay.

I doubt that there is a net advantage to the state, but if people would rather buy gambling chips than, say, have their teeth cleaned, perhaps we should give them this option. We should not, however, overlook the added costs to various state agencies who will help those who will become unable to pay for themselves because of what they paid to gamble.

Unless the huge plurality of gamblers are from out of state, we should be very wary of what Nevada promoters want to do for – or is it to – Connecticut.

ARLAND R. MEADE

Published: the Chronicle, Willimantic, Connecticut 4-17-1993

Esperanto: a Little Can Go a Long Way

Among the benefits of having the erudite, urbane Humphrey Tonkin as president of the University of Hartford is his interest in Esperanto. Mr. Tonkin speaks the international language and is a leader in encouraging others to learn it. This summer, the University of Hartford will be among the few institutions anywhere to offer a course in Esperanto. That's a nifty distinction.

Why learn Esperanto? Why take study time away from learning a "real" language, such as Spanish, which far more people speak and which has its own literature? The comparison is unfair. Esperanto, invented a century ago by a Polish physician, was meant to be a tool, a bridge between cultures. It is meant to be universal. No native language, including English, is.

Esperanto is also easier to learn than other languages. While fluency in any foreign tongue is an admirable goal, if its usage expands, Esperanto could be specifically suitable for travelers who just want to get by. Don't look for irregular verbs or silent letters or tricky accents that change not only inflection but meaning. Esperanto is drawn from many languages. But as its name implies – it bears the Latin root for "hope" – Esperanto will seem familiar enough to anyone acquainted with Romance and other European languages.

Esperanto can be especially useful as a middle ground, linguistically, between the citizens of two countries where languages with different alphabets or symbols are spoken – say English and Japanese, or French and Russian. Learning some Esperanto also invites speakers into what might be considered a worldwide club. People who speak it have an ice-breaker or excuse for contact with counterparts all over the globe.

The notion of a universal language promotes understanding and harmony. That's reason enough for everyone to learn to say bonan tagon – good day.

ARLAND R. MEADE

Published: the Hartford Courant 7-23-1991

The Enemy Is Us

We are selecting our nominees for the presidency as if we were selecting a Sunday school superintendent.

I'm sure there are a million citizens in each party who have never smoked pot, never been sexually unfaithful to their spouses, never drunk to excesses and, maybe, never made a mistake. And every one of them would be a useless president.

Would we be provoked if the media asked candidates to present evidence that they had been effective administrators? Or were students of history and government? Or showed intelligence when they have selected commissioners, advisors or whatever subordinates they have had to deal with?

Or what if the public showed concern about their attitudes on foreign policy, on handling the national debt, priorities on dealing with criminals, or, indeed, about the laws concerning criminals? And so on.

Would the media then ask such questions and insist on answers from the candidates? Why don't we look for character traits that would indicate ability to mediate, coordinate, stimulate, lead – instead of becoming hung up on whether a candidate acted a bit human two decades ago.

If we judged our presidents – whether Jefferson, Jackson, F.D. Roosevelt, Eisenhower, Kennedy and others – by the silly standards we are trying to judge our present candidates on, they may never have been elected and, likely, would have refused to run, as do many of our present national leaders. We'd be stupid to blame them for declining to run.

Our media feed our narrow interests; both we and the media are to blame. With one lifetime on earth, normal national leaders are declining to put themselves through the process we require for nomination.

We should not blame the candidates who try. We, the American voters, are truly our own enemy.

ARLAND R. MEADE

Published: Storrs Willimantic Chronicle 1988

www.ingramcontent.com/pod-product-compliance
Lightning Source LLC
Chambersburg PA
CBHW030342290526
45785CB00004B/1565